"I have known this man for mai
has impacted mine. James moves in a high realm of revelation
but writes in a very down-to-earth and practical way about
hearing God's voice. This foundational book will change your
life and equip you to help others in their walk with God."

Dr. Ché Ahn, apostle, Harvest Apostolic Center,
Pasadena, California; apostolic leader, HRock Church

"Some years ago, when we were looking for a prophetic voice to
bring to Nashville to help us learn to listen for God, we called
James Goll. We were not disappointed with his guidelines for
following hard after the voice of God. *Hearing God's Voice
Today* is an easy-to-read, easy-to-apply beginner's guide to
listening to God and discerning how God is speaking to you.
I find that it also has good reminders for those of us who have
been listening for a while."

Dr. Don Finto, founder, Caleb Company;
author, *Your People Shall Be My People*

"James Goll has lived a life of many years filled with the experience of hearing God's voice. All of us have much we can
learn from him, and this book gives all of us tips from one
who knows."

John Arnott, founding leader,
Catch the Fire, Toronto, Ontario, Canada

"If you have ever longed to hear God in a clearer way, *Hearing
God's Voice Today* is for you. James Goll has long had an intimate relationship with God and knows how to communicate
well what God has taught him. This book guides you in practical
and biblical ways in learning how to listen more closely. Fresh
insights he shares from recent experiences will make us desire to
listen more closely for the voice of the Holy Spirit with attentive
and expectant hearts. Thanks, James, for another great book!"

Quin Sherrer, co-author, *A Woman's Guide to Spiritual Warfare*

"I have known James Goll for almost thirty years. He was the first prophetic person I interviewed about how to hear from God. I have had James speak at many of my Voice of the Prophets conferences, and consider him to be a great source for learning about how to hear from God. He is a gifted prophetic minister and a great writer about the prophetic in all its aspects. You will learn and be blessed by James' book."

Dr. Randy Clark, overseer, Apostolic Network of Global
Awakening; author, *The Healing Breakthrough*

"Dr. James Goll is one of the most thorough teachers I know on prophetic topics. As an author, prophet and teacher, he delivers the word with an anointed blend of the academic and the mystical. The reader is always guaranteed to receive fresh 'manna' from the Spirit of God through his writings. *Hearing God's Voice Today* will surely bless, impact and establish you with keys for maturing in hearing, discerning and applying God's voice."

Patricia King, founder, Patricia King Ministries

"James Goll has that rare combination of being both prophet and teacher. He has helped multitudes with his strong prophetic gift and the clarity with which he hears from God. But his greater passion is equipping people to hear from God themselves. This book will help everyone who reads it to understand how God speaks so that they can have greater confidence in hearing God's voice and, ultimately, develop a closer relationship with Him. I highly recommend it!"

Stacey Campbell, author, *Ecstatic Prophecy*; co-founder, Be A Hero

"Keep this book close at hand. It's a volume you will refer to again and again. For those just learning to hear the voice of God, this book is packed with priceless teaching and practical application. For seasoned 'hearers,' this is a great reference work filled with spiritual principles and effective tools you can share with others. An excellent resource for the body of Christ. James Goll has done it again!"

Jane Hansen Hoyt, president/CEO, Aglow International

"How do we recognize the voice of God? This book is an excellent resource to better guide us in recognizing and responding to God's voice. James Goll is a mentor, prophet and teacher of impeccable character, and he has lived out this message through a powerful life testimony. *Hearing God's Voice Today* will leave you with a profound sense of faith, peace and confidence to venture further on your journey of listening—and becoming more productive in your calling."

Mahesh Chavda, Chavda Ministries International,
Charlotte, North Carolina; senior pastor, All Nations Church

"James Goll is truly one of the main 'fathers' of the modern-day prophetic movement! In *Hearing God's Voice Today*, James takes you through the 'School of the Spirit' and shows you how to work with the Holy Spirit to have a personal and intimate relationship with the One who is our tutor, who will 'guide us into all truth'! I was personally re-inspired to seek a fresher relationship with the Holy Spirit after reading this book."

Steve Shultz, founder, The Elijah List

"Few true believers will fulfill their destiny. Why? Because they have not learned to hear God's voice. This simple, biblical how-to book will revolutionize your walk with God!"

Sid Roth, host, *It's Supernatural!*

"Do you need to hear from the Lord? Do you feel the heavens have been silent for way too long? Position yourself to receive revelation and practical teaching as James Goll shares his own personal journey along with biblical insight in *Hearing God's Voice Today*."

Joni Lamb, co-founder, Daystar Television Network

"James Goll has been one of the main voices of prophetic inspiration and guidance that has affected my whole life and ministry. If there is a man who hears the voice of God, James Goll does. If there is a man who can write about it, James Goll can. This book will open up your heart and your ears to the rumbling voice of God."

Lou Engle, TheCall

"James Goll is a seasoned listener who operates in wisdom and revelation. He knows what the Lord's voice sounds like and what to do with what he hears. In *Hearing God's Voice Today*, James equips believers in all stages of their walk with God to hear His voice more and more clearly. He shares practical insights and principles for developing ears that hear what the Spirit of God says. If you want more certainty God is speaking to you, this book will help instill confidence in your heart."

Jennifer LeClaire, senior editor, *Charisma* magazine; author, *The Making of a Prophet*; director, Awakening House of Prayer

HEARING
GOD'S
Voice
TODAY

HEARING GOD'S Voice TODAY

PRACTICAL HELP FOR LISTENING TO HIM
AND RECOGNIZING HIS VOICE

James W. Goll

Chosen
a division of Baker Publishing Group
Minneapolis, Minnesota

© 2004, 2008, 2016 by James Goll

Published by Chosen Books
Minneapolis, Minnesota
www.chosenbooks.com

Chosen Books is a division of
Baker Publishing Group, Grand Rapids, Michigan

ISBN 978-0-8007-9813-0

Library of Congress Control Number: 2016931361

Previously published by Regal Books as *The Beginner's Guide to Hearing God*

Printed in the United States of America

Library of Congress Cataloging-in-Publication Data

Unless otherwise indicated, Scripture quotations are from the New American Standard Bible®, copyright © 1960, 1962, 1963, 1968, 1971, 1972, 1973, 1975, 1977, 1995 by The Lockman Foundation. Used by permission. (www.Lockman.org)

Scripture quotations identified NKJV are from the New King James Version®. Copyright © 1982 by Thomas Nelson, Inc. Used by permission. All rights reserved.

Scripture quotations identified NIV are from the Holy Bible, New International Version®. NIV®. Copyright © 1973, 1978, 1984, 2011 by Biblica, Inc.™ Used by permission of Zondervan. All rights reserved worldwide. www.zondervan.com

Scripture quotations identified NLT are from the *Holy Bible*, New Living Translation, copyright © 1996, 2004, 2015 by Tyndale House Foundation. Used by permission of Tyndale House Publishers, Inc., Carol Stream, Illinois 60188. All rights reserved.

Scripture quotations identified KJV are from the King James Version of the Bible.

Cover design by Rob Williams, InsideOutCreativeArts

Baker Publishing Group publications use paper produced from sustainable forestry practices and post-consumer waste whenever possible.

With an overflowing heart of thanksgiving, I wish to dedicate this book to two of my mentors in hearing God's voice. The Holy Spirit brought these two gifted men into my life, and they have made a dramatic impact on my destiny.

Years ago, Mahesh Chavda, of All Nations Church in Fort Mill, South Carolina, taught me some of his best-kept secrets about hearing God. I watched, I listened and I learned from a man who spent time with God.

May the Lord reward you, Mahesh.

I also wish to acknowledge and give honor to my "prophetic papa," the late Bob Jones. This dear, gifted man took me under his wing in the early years of the prophetic movement. Bob was a "seer of seers" in modern Christianity.

Thank You, Lord, for Your gift to me in Bob Jones.

Contents

Foreword

Idon't know many people with more experience in prayer and intercession combined with years of prophetic ministry than James Goll. He is a general in the Kingdom, and I have been privileged to know him for close to twenty years. In his newest book, *Hearing God's Voice Today*, James goes back to the roots of his ministry and leads us on a journey into hearing the heart of the Lord.

Much like learning to walk as a baby, listening to the voice of God is a skill that can be developed through teaching, instruction and practice. You first learn to crawl, take a step and fall down, get back up and, with perseverance and determination, take some more steps. Eventually you find yourself running a race to win! As my friend James expresses it, you can take entry-level classes and graduate to higher levels of learning in the School of Hearing the Voice of God.

In spite of the increasing fascination and intrigue of many with the dark side of the supernatural with psychics and palm readers, James reminds us that there is a growing hunger for authentic, real spiritual encounters. Most people are simply unaware that God has designed a way of reaching through the veil of eternity to communicate with His beloved people. But He has an answer, and this book is full of some of the Holy Spirit's tools to assist you.

Do you want to accomplish your destiny and have a clear understanding of your calling, anointing and gifting? Then look no further. James has done a masterful job of communicating in a simple, understandable way some of the practical steps to hearing God's voice today. He doesn't just honor the God of yesterday, but teaches us how to have a greater hunger to hear God's voice now.

The foundational revelation in this book will open the door to new dimensions of your relationship with God. It is a must-read for every Christian who longs to hear the Lord's voice and be transformed into the image of Christ in order to change the world.

Don't miss out! You can be part of the growing community of believers who hear the wonderful words of life and learn to share them with others.

> Kris Vallotton, co-founder,
> Bethel School of Supernatural Ministry;
> author, *The Supernatural Ways of Royalty*,
> *Spirit Wars* and many more;
> leader, Bethel Church, Redding, California

Acknowledgments

Deep gratitude goes to the past and present staff at Encounters Network, formerly called Ministry to the Nations, for their support in every project I undertake. My personal Prayer Shield faithfully intercedes, holding up my hands, for which I am thankful. I am forever grateful to my dear family, who stands by my side, cheering me on.

I also wish to thank my friend Quin Sherrer, who opened the door for the initial publishing of the original manuscript of this book with Servant Publications/Vine Books. Later, the book became a part of the Beginner's Guide series that was adopted into the Regal Books family. There, it went through two revisions, as well. Kathy Deering became my consistent mainstay as my writing and editing assistant through all of these transitions. Kathy has been a gift from God to my life, and thus to yours.

Eventually, the book was reenvisioned and reshaped by my longtime publishing friends at Baker/Chosen Books into this book you hold in your hands now, *Hearing God's Voice Today*. What started out as my shortest book for beginners has been flipped into a marvelous book full of Scriptures, stories and practical tools meant to help anyone at any point or time in their life in order to help them cultivate a closer relationship with God.

Introduction

God Still Speaks Today

God still speaks today! Are you listening? What are you hearing? Is your faith growing as a result of your interpersonal communion with God? While we agree that the canon of Scripture is closed, we also believe that Jesus Christ is the same yesterday, today and forever (see Hebrews 13:8). What He did before, He continues to do. God has spoken, God speaks and God promises to continue to speak to us.

One of the ongoing activities of the Holy Spirit is listening and then communicating. The Holy Spirit speaks to us what He hears: "But when He, the Spirit of truth, comes, He will guide you into all the truth; for He will not speak on His own initiative, but whatever He hears, He will speak; and He will disclose to you what is to come" (John 16:13).

One of the most overlooked ministries of the Holy Spirit is that of listening, as He listens before He speaks. We need to take some lessons from the nature and character of the Holy Spirit, it seems to me!

Let's take a quick look at this Old Testament verse quoted by Jesus in the New Testament:

He *humbled* you and let you be *hungry*, and *fed* you with manna which you did not know, nor did your fathers know, that He might make you *understand* that man does not live by bread alone, but man lives by everything that proceeds out of the mouth of the LORD.

Deuteronomy 8:3, emphasis added

The first half of this verse is essential to grasp in order to receive the promise stated in the second half. Look at these progressive steps: first comes humility; second comes hunger; third comes being fed fresh manna; and last, you are made to understand.

Spiritual hunger is what it is all about. Are you hungry for God and His ever-proceeding word? It is the hungry who are fed things they formerly knew nothing about. There are always new things to learn from God. There are always new things in God's heart He wants to share with His people.

Satan himself confronted Jesus, and Jesus overcame the devil by declaring the written Word of God. Matthew 4:4 states, "But He [Jesus] answered and said, 'It is written, "Man shall not live on bread alone, but on every word that proceeds out of the mouth of God."'"

You see, man lives by the ever-proceeding word of the Lord. God has spoken. God speaks and God will continue to speak in the future. This requires a listening relationship on man's part—one like the Holy Spirit has with the Father and the Son.

This is why I composed this practical and, I trust, inspirational book, *Hearing God's Voice Today*. I wanted to give you some of the practical yet personal tips that have been given to me.

Are you listening? God is still speaking today!

Blessings to you in Christ Jesus,

James W. Goll

1

As It Was in the Beginning

"My sheep hear My voice, and I know them, and
they follow Me."

John 10:27

"Behold, I stand at the door and knock; if anyone
hears My voice and opens the door, I will come in
to him and will dine with him, and he with Me."

Revelation 3:20

Does God really speak today? Will He speak personally to
me? If I listen, will He speak in such a manner that even
I can understand? Thank God, the answer is yes! And, believe
it or not (I expect you will believe it by the time you finish this
book), God Himself wants all of us to hear what He is saying—more than any of us do!

Each of us was created with a deep inner longing to hear our
Master's voice. He did not make us to be mechanical robots

that just march around, doing preordained things. Our Father God created us to have fellowship with Him. It is our birthright to have an actual relationship with our God.

If our yearning for an intimate relationship with the lover of our souls is to be fulfilled, hearing His voice is a must. We cannot grow in our relationship with God unless we draw near to Him, trusting that He wants to speak to us personally.

Jesus came to restore humankind into the sweet fellowship that Adam and Eve first had known in the Garden. Sin cut them off from God, and they could no longer be close to God. Sin, in the same way today, cuts off each of us from God. But sin does not have the final word. Because of the cross and the shed blood of Christ Jesus, we can be restored to fellowship. One of the main reasons Jesus came was to enable us to walk in restored communion with God.

From my perspective, the greatest need in the Church today is for believers to clearly hear the voice of God for themselves. For us to reach our potential for an intimate relationship with God, we must be able to communicate with Him. Communication with God goes two ways: (1) talking to Him and (2) listening to Him when He talks to us. To have good communication, we must learn how and when to speak up and how to push the pause button in order to listen.

Most of us seem to do okay on the first one. But we have to take the time to learn the second one, the lost art of listening to Him expectantly.

It Takes Two

Fellowship is not a one-way road. It takes at least two, with both parties—in one another's presence—sharing attentively in some kind of communion. Our relationship with our heavenly Papa was never meant to be a long-distance telephone conversation.

"Available" is God's middle name. He is just aching to spend time alone with each of us. He yearns to hear from us. He wants us to know how attentive He is.

A lot of things have changed over my forty-plus years in full-time vocational ministry. I was often away from my beloved family for days at a time, but I diligently attempted to keep in touch with what was happening at home. Sometimes I did a better job than at other times. Using wonderful modern technology—cell phones, email, texting and such—my late wife, Michal Ann, and I attempted to keep in touch. But phone calls and email messages did not compare to or replace being with my dear wife and family. Sometimes I just needed a hug! True love requires being together. The greatest key to hearing God's voice is cultivating a love-based relationship.

Mark Virkler states it this way: "The voice of God, I've discovered, is Spirit-to-spirit communication, the Holy Spirit speaking directly to my spirit."[1] True fellowship requires that both parties speak and listen, both sharing their hearts deeply with one another. This is the key to keeping all relationships fresh and alive. In an atmosphere of trust, we share our heart with someone else. Communion with God is much more than a ritual or "information time." It is Spirit-to-spirit time!

Dutch Sheets said, "What topic could possibly deserve more of our attention than listening to God? When the source of all life and wisdom speaks, those who would be wise listen. The foolish either don't care to or don't learn how. The fruit of both is the same: destructive ignorance."[2] We do not want to walk in the path of destruction but in the path of life. *Oh, God, deliver us from formulaic Christianity, and restore to us the pathways of constant dependency. Teach us the ways of life. Teach us to live transparent, shared lives.*

As for me, I want to hear His voice and intimately know Him, not just on a casual basis, but also on a daily, vibrant one. Join me and thousands of others who are learning to hear the Master's beckoning voice by leaning our ears toward Him. Come with me now on a journey of beginning to hear (and love hearing) God's voice.

How It Began with Me

By the grace of God and the influence of my praying mother and church community, I grew up knowing that Jesus was my best friend. As a child, I would go on long walks in rural Missouri and just talk continuously to God. Often, while gazing into the skies, I would listen to see if He had anything to say back.

As the youngest child, with two older sisters, I always had wanted a brother. So Jesus became the brother I never had. Years passed, and I graduated from high school. But one thing remained the same: Jesus was right there with me as my close friend.

At college, I hungered for more of God. This quest led me into divine collision with a group of people with whom this straitlaced, rural Methodist kid did not have much in common—the Jesus People. When I got filled with the Holy Spirit and released into His gifts in the Jesus Movement, it was like my little black-and-white TV set turned into OmniVision overnight. I was absolutely transformed.

Suddenly, my life was very different. I had attempted to walk with the Lord all along, but now my life in the Spirit took a quantum leap. Somehow I had been able to detect His voice before, but in comparison to what I had previously experienced, now it was as if God had just given me a hearing aid. I really did not know what to do with all this stuff—impressions, mental snapshots, hunches, knowledge, short thoughts and full phrases—that were being released into my heart and mind. But the Holy Spirit became an awesome tutor to me on this immense learning curve.

Still being quite young in this realm, I thought all believers lived this way. I thought that at last I was living the normal Christian life. (And I still think it is supposed to be that way!) I did not realize how many believers could not point to one single instance of hearing God's voice for themselves. Yet even with my heightened experience of God, I knew I needed more if I was to really advance in maturity in hearing and knowing His voice.

A Desire for Discernment

In the middle of my junior year at Central Missouri State University, this drive to know God led me to cry out for discernment. Late one night, I went to pray with another Jesus freak in an Episcopal church where a friend's father, an evangelical, Spirit-filled Episcopal priest, was the rector. I loved sneaking away when I could to spend time there in quiet reflection, as His sweet presence seemed to reside there. At the front of the sanctuary, on the wall close to the Communion rail, was a lighted candle. It was a symbolic representation of the light of God and presence of God.

While basking in the light of God's presence late that night, I began to vocalize my desire to hear and know the voice of God better. I proceeded logically, telling God:

Based on John 10:27, You have stated, "My sheep hear My voice, and I know them, and they follow Me." Now, I don't have any problem with the first part of the verse, "My sheep hear My voice." I know I have heard Your voice, because in Revelation 3:20, it says, "Behold, I stand at the door and knock; if anyone hears My voice and opens the door, I will come in to him and will dine with him, and he with Me." I have heard Your knock at the door of my heart, and I am one of Yours.

I continued with my line-by-line presentation:

So, Father, I accept by faith that I do hear Your voice. The second part of the verse, I don't have any problem with either. I know that You know me, and You know me better than I know myself. I don't have any problem with that. But it's the third part of that verse that I have a big problem with: "And they follow Me." So, God, I need to do more than just hear Your voice—because I also hear my voice, the voice of my flesh, the voices of others, the voice of the world and the voice of the enemy, Satan. Therefore, if I'm going to be able to follow You, I must do more than only hear Your voice. I need to be able to discern Your voice from the other voices.

That night, my friend and I knelt in prayer and simply said, "Lord, we ask that You enroll us in Your School of the Spirit. Teach us not only how to hear but also how to discern Your voice from the voice of the stranger and all the other voices that contend for our attention. Please do this so that we can truly follow You."

Perhaps there is a book in heaven called the Book of Godly Desires in which God keeps records. All I know is that night, in November 1972, it seemed to me the Lord wrote down my name in His book. I enrolled in His School of the Spirit. Forty-plus years later, I am still taking various classes in that school. I don't think I have graduated from it yet. I want to be among those who are continually learning how to hear and discern His wonderful voice and how to follow Him.

How about you?

Lessons from the Original Couple

A good starting place in this School of the Spirit is the lessons we can learn from the original couple, Adam and Eve, as recorded in Genesis 3. After they tasted the forbidden fruit, God came looking for some fellowship with Adam and Eve—to walk and talk with them (as He does with you and me). In *The Coming Prophetic Revolution*, which was later revised to *The Lifestyle of a Prophet*, I wrote about what this must have been like:

> Can you imagine, after Adam and Eve had known God, and He knew them, how quickly the spiritual climate changed? As a result of their disobedience, they experienced instantaneous barriers to their intimacy with Him. Walls shot up. After their sin they plucked off leaves from the nearest bush as quickly as they could and sewed coverings for themselves. They were hiding from the Lord their Creator for the first time in their lives.
>
> But God, in His passionate pursuit, was still drawing close. A new reaction stirred within them as He drew near. Previously they had run toward the sound of His footsteps. Now they ran in the opposite direction. Before, their response had been for joy: "Oh, wow, it's Father!" Now it was dread and fear: "Oh, no, it's Father!" They were guilt-ridden. Never had they had such an emotional reaction or even such a thought before! They had not known condemnation or fear or shame. Now, as a result of their disobedience, they ran and hid from the voice of God.[3]

This pretty well sums up the difference between the joy of hearing God and obeying His voice and the dilemma of hearing God's voice and *not* obeying. Big difference!

Here's the good news: God is searching for us. He is drawing near—whether we want Him to or not! He is the glorious intruder. God does not give up on His beloved; He wants to walk and talk with you. But there can be some sad news also: Barriers to intimacy result when we choose to ignore what He tells us. So let's listen up and learn. We need Him. We need to hear His voice. Let's cultivate a heart and life that responds when He speaks.

Lessons from the Pioneer

Many pilgrims of the faith have walked this path before us. We can look to them and learn from both their failures and their successes. They needed to hear God in their day, just as we do in ours. And God drew near to them in His loving grace, just as He will draw near to us.

With this in mind, let's look at the life of Abraham, who is called the father and pioneer of our faith. This man heard impossible promises from God, things that would require God's presence for their fulfillment. (By the way, a good test of whether we have heard God speak is that He rarely asks us to do something we can do in our own strength or by our own effort. God does not want to give us a mere word. He wants to create a constant need in us for more of Him!)

Abraham had to feel rather desperate and dependent, don't you think? God required everything of him. Through miraculous intervention, the promised son finally was born—in Abraham's old age. But when this precious son, Isaac, reached early manhood, God spoke to Abraham again and told him to take his son and offer him as a sacrifice on Mount Moriah (see Genesis 22:1–2). What a test! But Abraham obeyed, and what an outcome! At the zero hour, God supplied a ram that could be sacrificed in place of Isaac, and God was satisfied. This makes Abraham our finest example of believing God and obeying Him fully.

Have you ever had to learn the grace of yielding? Have you ever wanted to hold on too tightly to every little bit you have? I know I have. But as I see more of the revelation of God's great love for me, I, like Abraham, eventually melt and yield to His Kingdom ways. So will you as you, too, learn to walk this pilgrimage of faith.

Abraham was called the friend of God (see 2 Chronicles 20:7). How did he become God's friend? Maybe by being with Him so much. Abraham became familiar with God's voice, and he learned to recognize even God's shadow when He was walking past.

I, too, want to be the friend of God. In fact, that is what I think hearing God's voice is all about.

We Have a Desperate Need

Many other people in the Bible are examples for us of how to maintain a personal relationship with God. As distinctly different as they are in personality and circumstances, they all show us a desperate face. Oh, to be like Moses, who talked to God face-to-face. (*But please, Lord, save me from forty years of wilderness wandering!*) If we want to hear God in the gentle breeze, as Elijah did, then we must be aware it might involve getting the moody blues and hiding out in a cave. If we want angelic encounters, like Daniel had, then we must get ready for the fire of God's furnace, as well. If we want to do the impossible, we must respond as simply as a young teenaged girl named Mary responded when she received the words of an angel and conceived a gift from God. (*But, God, that was a onetime deal, right?*) Or we must be like Paul, the amazing apostle, who recognized that the words he heard from the Lord were given to prepare him for the costs that lay ahead.

There are scores of others, of course. They may seem famous to us now, but Abraham, Moses, Mary and Paul were only ordinary people like us. Each person ever created has a need and a longing to hear our Creator's voice. Each person can talk to

God, and we can hear Him, too. Each person is created with the need to be continuously dependent on His voice. I think of the words of an old hymn: "I need Thee, oh, I need Thee; every hour I need Thee."

We all need to hear and know the voice of our Father, the voice of the Son, Jesus, and that of the Holy Spirit, our Helper, Guide and Comforter. All three desire to speak to us. It is all about being in God's presence.

The veteran teacher and author Fuchsia Pickett wrote:

> We must enter into unity with God's will for our lives through divine revelation. Christ wants our minds to think His thoughts and our wills to choose His will to be performed in and through us. [This happens as] we cultivate our relationship with Christ.[4]

Perhaps you, too, will add your name to the list of those who heard God speak and then became strong in faith, doing mighty exploits in His great name. Remember, "faith comes by hearing" (Romans 10:17 NKJV). Take time to listen for His voice with all your heart.

Are you ready to get started with a few lessons?

You Can Start Now

You don't have to wait any longer—classes start every day! School is in session at all times. You can enroll right now and be a student with me in the School of the Spirit, where we learn to hear the voice of God. If this echoes the cry of your heart, pray:

Dear Lord, I want to hear Your voice and learn Your ways. Be my teacher and guide. Enroll me in the School of the Spirit, and teach me to hear Your voice. Write down my name! I want to know You, to be a disciple of Christ Jesus and to have sweet communion with You. I want to hear

You, have more faith and obey what You tell me. Help, Lord, for Your servant wants to listen. Amen.

THINK ABOUT IT

1. If we are satisfied and content with the status quo of our spiritual lives, we will never try very hard to hear God's voice. But when we are desperate for guidance or reassurance, we will hasten to consult Him. On a scale of 1 to 10, how desperate are you to hear God's voice? (The 1 represents complete satisfaction with your present life, and the 10 means you feel trapped and stuck and that you would do just about anything to be able to hear from Him.)

   1   2   3   4   5   6   7   8   9   10

2. Have you ever heard God's voice? What did it sound like? Were you aware at first that it was the voice of God?

2

The Holy Spirit at Work Today

"But I tell you the truth, it is to your advantage that I go away; for if I do not go away, the Helper will not come to you; but if I go, I will send Him to you."

John 16:7

"However, when He, the Spirit of truth, has come, He will guide you into all truth; for He will not speak on His own authority, but whatever He hears He will speak; and He will tell you things to come."

John 16:13 NKJV

"When the Helper comes, whom I will send to you from the Father, that is the Spirit of truth who proceeds from the Father, He will testify about Me."

John 15:26

Our Papa God has many gifts to give to us. The biggest gift of all, of course, is His Son, Jesus—yes, Jesus, the beloved Son, who, through the work of the cross, purchased for us our salvation, redemption, atonement from our sins and eternal life and promised to be our Bridegroom that great Day in the future. Our heavenly Father gave us His very heart in that one gift. Jesus is the greatest gift of all.

Jesus, in turn, gives us the wonderful gifts of His love, which include promises (that He will keep!), cleansing, hope, healing, deliverance, hugs, kisses and lots of other good things, all of which come from the heart of His Father. The gift of Jesus' shed blood alone, with all the power and love that it carries, is beyond our understanding.

Additionally, Father and Son have sent their best by giving each of us disciples one very special gift, a gift that keeps giving us more gifts. What could that be? It is our Comforter, our Guide, the One called to be alongside us to help us out—the Holy Spirit. The Holy Spirit allows us to sense our Father God's personal, loving touch. Getting to know what His touch feels like is a lifelong adventure.

The Third Person of the Godhead

Although I loved and accepted Christ as my personal Savior at a very young age, for many years the Holy Spirit was just a ghost to me. That is what the Apostles' Creed that I recited in church every Sunday stated so simply: "I believe in the Holy Ghost." I don't remember much else being taught about this third Person of the Godhead in the rural Protestant church where I was reared. I knew that He was not Casper the Friendly Ghost, but I wasn't quite sure who He really was or what He came to do. Jesus I knew as my friend; I was getting used to God as my Father. But who was this Holy Ghost?

It all remained a bit of a mystery—until I ran into some wild Jesus fanatics! They sang strange songs, such as "The Holy Ghost Will Set Your Feet A-Dancing." (Huh? He will do *what*? With *whom*? Not me, dude!) As time went on, I fell even more in love with Jesus and also grew fanatical about the things of the Holy Spirit. He quickly became one of my closest companions.

Today, the Holy Spirit indeed is my friend, partner, guide and co-conspirator. He wants to be yours, as well. But to get close to Him, you may have to push through misconceptions, spiritual warfare, debates about religious theories and a bunch of just plain old opposition, until you come to the place where you and He are rightly related with one another and on good speaking terms.

My friend Quin Sherrer and her co-author, Ruthanne Garlock, wrote:

What an extraordinary gift the Father bestowed upon his children when he sent the Holy Spirit to be our helper! Is it any wonder that Satan tries to minimize the significance of the gift and divide and confuse the body of Christ concerning it?[1]

The late evangelist David Wilkerson, founder of Teen Challenge, adds the following timeless insight:

Give much quality time to communion with the Holy Spirit. He will not speak to anyone who is in a hurry. All of God's Word is about waiting on Him! . . . Wait patiently. Seek the Lord and minister praises to Him. Take authority over every other voice that whispers thoughts to you. Believe that the Spirit is greater than these, and that He will not let you be deceived or blind. Be willing to set your heart on Him.[2]

Many Christians know a lot about the Holy Spirit. They write great, detailed books and go into the Greek lexicon to explain

Him. They quote the Old Testament and the New Testament. Some can instruct us by descriptively defining all of His diverse functions. All of this is valuable.

But in the midst of all of it, stop and ask yourself, *Do I really, really know the Holy Spirit as a person, as someone with whom I am becoming intimate? Is He really my friend, my helper, my comforter and my guide?* Even if you feel you cannot honestly say that you know the Holy Spirit yet, remember that a love relationship is a two-way street. He is right beside you, waiting to be entreated. He is waiting to be engaged.

The Tutor of God's Personal Touch

The Holy Spirit is our counselor and our teacher, yet He is more than a teacher. He is more like a tutor—but He is not just any tutor. He is the kind of tutor who truly loves to spend individual, personal time with each of His students. He is like that rare kind of guidance counselor who actually becomes a friend. He is like the teacher who becomes a personal mentor.

I respect the Spirit highly as a good teacher. But I have such warm affection for Him as my personal tutor. I never had that for any other teacher or, in some ways, for any earthly friend.

To help us gain a little more insight on the subject, let's glance at how the word *tutor* is described in the dictionary:

tutor *n*: a person charged with the instruction and guidance of another as a private teacher

tutor *vt* 1: to have guardianship, tutelage, or care of 2: to teach or guide usually individually in a special subject or for a particular purpose : COACH ~ *vi* 1: to do the work of a tutor 2: to receive instruction especially privately[3]

Here we see more of the potential for the special kind of relationship we can have with the Holy Spirit. As a personal tutor, He is also a personal coach who can help us win out on the playing field of life.

In addition—great news!—He is not like an ordinary tutor or teacher who clocks in and out. As we graduate from one level of spiritual development to the next, He remains our lifelong personal tutor. We start with the best, and we end with the best. As we end our days here on earth, He even prepares us for our postgraduate course in life hereafter. All along, He instructs us as to what life lessons we need to learn, and He even helps us know in what order to take them.

When asked the question, What one person in your life has influenced you the most?, often people answer with the name of a special schoolteacher or coach they had when growing up. I know what my answer would be. Besides Jesus Himself, the Holy Spirit has made more of an impact on my life than any person has.

The Holy Spirit leaves an immeasurable impact upon our lives. He is able to teach, influence and comfort—all at the same time, always with the most careful love. Jesus loves us, this we know, but the Holy Spirit shows us that God even *likes* us! God, in the person of the Holy Spirit, likes hanging out with us, and we with Him.

The quality of the time we spend fellowshiping with the Holy Spirit has everything to do with hearing God's voice. I love to ask Him questions. My mother always said I was a very curious child. With God, we all can be curious cats. Go ahead and ask Him questions. The more specific we become in our asking, the more detailed His answers to us will be.

In fact, pause right now and ask God a question. He will answer! Watch out, though. The Holy Spirit might turn around and ask *you* some questions, and perhaps even give you some tests to take.

The Teacher of Many Classes

God offers tremendous classes in His School of the Spirit. Our personal tutor specializes in teaching subjects not found in worldly institutions—because He has something more in mind than merely imparting knowledge to us. He tutors to transform lives! He offers classes like Holiness 101, which, of course, is followed by Fire of Holiness 102. After we get a fresh grip on holiness (or it gets a grip on us!), we jump up into Victorious Living 201 and Miracles 202. Maybe, eventually, we will graduate into upper-level classes, such as Humility 301 and Death to Self 302.

Another dimension of the Holy Spirit's instruction in His school is that we will be impacted by His revelatory teaching grace. With Him at our elbow, we learn to dissect the Word of God instead of frogs. Instead of learning how to diagram sentences or describe verbs and their tenses, He introduces us to the Author of the Word of God, launching us on an eternity-spanning exploration.

One of His tutorial specialties is one of my favorites: a class on foreign languages (the gift of speaking in tongues). Admittance is open to anyone who has taken the prerequisite class, Salvation 101. After that, we have another related course, called Interpretation of Tongues 102, where our Guide not only enables us to pray in a language we don't have to study in the traditional way, but also gives us ongoing help to translate what we have prayed.

So it goes. Furthermore, all of these lessons hone our study skills. We get better and better at hearing the voice of God today. (Our personal Tutor is quite interested in that part!)

By the way, history classes are an important area of expertise for the Holy Spirit. His slant on history is entirely accurate. It is not biased, nor does it favor any one economic group, nationality or political view. All of life is actually His story.

Through these history classes, He teaches us how we fit into the big picture; He builds our personal history with God. While meeting our needs for the present moment, He establishes something permanent in us for the future in His unshakable Kingdom. Thus, we are prepared for the real world, the eternal world, where things that really matter include faith, hope, compassion and, above all, true love. We learn that holiness, righteousness and honesty are far more important than reading the stock market and that sacrificial giving is foundational if we want our life story to show that we have followed in Jesus' footsteps.

The School of the Future

We find another branch of God's School of the Spirit in what I call God's School of the Future. Can you imagine a class in which the teacher actually knows the future—a professor who can teach history before it happens? The Holy Spirit knows it all. He even knows everything about you! He is omniscient. He sometimes releases preview clips of things to come. As a part of His job description as our personal coach, He gives us cheat sheets by illuminating a Bible passage, imparting dreams and unfolding visions. He dispenses vignettes of things that are about to take place while preparing us for what lies ahead. Now, He does not tell us everything, or we would not need the commodities called faith and trust. It is all quite amazing.

To take you into the School of the Future, I am going to take you into a lesson from my past. Yesterday's dream about your tomorrow becomes your opportunity to experience God today!

I distinctly remember one Sunday morning in May 1975, when I was 22 years old. I was taking one of my regular prayer walks with God, strolling through Pertle Springs Park in Warrensburg, Missouri. Actually voicing the question aloud, as though I was talking with a friend walking beside me, I asked, "Who's for me?" To my utter amazement, an immediate reply came right into my heart and mind: *Ann Willard*. Somewhat startled, I stuttered, "Who?" Again it came: *Ann Willard*. I reacted at this point and said, "Well, the last I knew, she was practically engaged to some guy studying to be a Methodist pastor. Who?" Once more, the affirming voice of the Lord echoed in the chambers of my heart: *Ann Willard*. And then He continued, saying, *Not only that, but by September you will be outwardly engaged, and the following May 15, you will be married.*

I must admit, I liked this news. In fact, I was elated. Ann and I had worked at the local hospital together the summer before and had enjoyed each other's company.

As far-fetched as it might sound, it all occurred exactly as it had been spoken. Within four months, Ann Willard and I were outwardly engaged. And on Saturday, May 15, 1976, we were wed. (By the way, our marriage was full of friendship, love and good fruit. We had the lovely joy of being united for 32 years. We birthed four miraculous children and traveled the world together. But in the fall of 2008, after a long battle with cancer, Michal Ann slipped through the thin veil, into the other side. She now worships the Lord in heaven while I carry on here, on the earth side.)

I wish hearing God's voice was always that dramatic and easy. It is not. But sometimes it is! Whatever the case, before jumping to rash conclusions and making some ridiculous blunder, please hold on long enough to read the rest of this book. This I know with assurance: He is the God of the past, the present and the future. As we hold His hand in a posture of trust and dependency, we can successfully walk the path less chosen, the one on which we are led by His Holy Spirit in every detail of our lives—yesterday, today and tomorrow.

He is the Spirit of truth, and He always points us in the right direction—toward truth. The Holy Spirit not only gives us a revelation of truth, but He also builds truthfulness into the depths of our personality. We become like Him as we spend time with Him. His characteristics are imparted to us. They rub off on us, just as we see happen in our close relationships. Having the standard of truthfulness built into our lives drops a plumb line into our character, which enables us not only to hear but also to discern the voice of God today.

Along with truth, our Helper is willing and able to build into the fabric of our being the many other attributes of God's character. As our tutor, He has a personal interest in seeing us grow to express what God is like as we live out what we hear Him saying.

The Advantage Given to Us

Have you ever needed to know which way to turn—what choice to make? Ever feel like you are caught in that awful position called *transition*, where you wonder if things will ever move forward and change? Don't you sometimes wish a complete guidebook or DVD would just drop down from heaven's storehouse, into your lap? Have you sometimes wished for a personal appointment with the man Christ Jesus, so He could tell you everything you want to know?

But Jesus said, "It is to your advantage that I go away; for if I do not go away, the Helper will not come to you; but if I go, I will send Him to you" (John 16:7). Jesus, the Son of God, who cannot lie, told His disciples that it is better that the Holy

Spirit come and be with them than for Him to remain. Jesus had more things to say to His disciples, but they could not bear them right then. He knew ahead of time that they would need some ongoing coaching. He also knew He would have a lot more disciples to tutor in the centuries to come. So the Master enacted a grand plan: He would go back to His Father, and they would send the Holy Spirit to the twelve disciples, to the other believers who were with them and to all subsequent disciples.

That is what He did. After Jesus died, He was buried and rose from the dead. He ascended into heaven. Then, on the Day of Pentecost, the very breath of God came as a mighty wind with tongues of fire. The rest we know as part of Church history. We are witnesses of the fact that our Father God, through Jesus Christ, is still blowing that same Pentecost fire around the world and imparting His Spirit to us today.

God has promised in His Word that He will take care of us and never leave us or forsake us. He knows that when it comes to walking into the shadows of the unknown, we much prefer to hold someone's hand and be guided by the voice of a wise and strong guide. That is why our Father gave us our very own personal tutor—His precious Holy Spirit. You see, the Holy Spirit is alive and well, continuing the work of our Father God today!

Isaiah the prophet declared, "Your ears will hear a word behind you, 'This is the way, walk in it,' whenever you turn to the right or to the left" (Isaiah 30:21). Let's begin to tune in to hear His voice today.

Father, I present myself to You in Jesus Christ's name. I declare that the Holy Spirit is alive and active in my life today. Draw me closer to Your heart so I can hear what the Spirit is saying. I ask that the Holy Spirit be my personal tutor, guide and teacher. I want to take more classes in Your School of the Spirit. Lead me. Guide me. Teach me how to listen more effectively, in Jesus Christ's name. Amen and amen!

THINK ABOUT IT

1. Have you entered into the Spirit-filled life? If not, stop everything and throw yourself into your Savior's arms. Tell Him you want to be entirely His. Ask Him for the gift of His Holy Spirit. He will not disappoint you.

2. Which of the Holy Spirit's special classes are you taking at this time? Are you going through some hard times? Are you enjoying some new opportunities to minister to others? What sets of Scriptures are personally meaningful to you right now? (By the way, don't worry if you seem to repeat some of the lessons you learn. That seems to be part of the normal Christian life.)

3

The Sound of Many Rushing Waters

Then I turned to see the voice that was speaking with me. And having turned I saw seven golden lampstands; and in the middle of the lampstands I saw one like a son of man, clothed in a robe reaching to the feet, and girded across His chest with a golden sash. His head and His hair were white like white wool, like snow; and His eyes were like a flame of fire. His feet were like burnished bronze, when it has been made to glow in a furnace, and His voice was like the sound of many waters.

Revelation 1:12–15

Behold, an angel of the Lord appeared to Joseph in a dream, and said, "Get up! Take the Child and His mother and flee to Egypt, and remain there until I tell you; for Herod is going to search for the Child to destroy Him."

Matthew 2:13

> And the LORD opened the mouth of the donkey, and she said to Balaam, "What have I done to you, that you have struck me these three times?" . . . Then the LORD opened the eyes of Balaam, and he saw the angel of the LORD standing in the way with his drawn sword in his hand; and he bowed all the way to the ground.
>
> Numbers 22:28, 31

> But He answered and said, "It is written, 'Man shall not live on bread alone, but on every word that proceeds out of the mouth of God.'"
>
> Matthew 4:4

After Jesus' forty-day fast, when He was being tempted, Satan said, "If You are the Son of God, command that these stones become bread" (Matthew 4:3). Jesus answered by quoting Deuteronomy 8:3: "Man does not live by bread alone, but man lives by everything that proceeds out of the mouth of the LORD." The word *proceeds*, also found in Matthew 4:4, is a continuous-action verb. God's life-giving word proceeds and continues to proceed. It is God's ever-proceeding word that gives us life! God has spoken; God is speaking; God will continue to guide His children by speaking.

God has also said that out of the "mouth of two or three witnesses every fact may be confirmed" (Matthew 18:16). For emphasis, we find this statement, or a variation of it, three times in Scripture: in Deuteronomy 19:15, in Matthew 18:16 and in 2 Corinthians 13:1. Evidently, God wants us to hear His voice, discern it from other voices and then, through the spirit of wisdom and revelation, correctly interpret and apply the word He has spoken to us.

God does not want us to know only the historical Jesus, who came in human form and walked among men. He yearns for us also to know the living, resurrected Christ through the power of the Holy Spirit. The Father wants to enable us to hear, know and obey the risen Lord.

But often we don't realize He is speaking to us. And no wonder we miss His cues—His voice is like the sound of many rushing waters! Revelation 1:15 says, "His voice was like the sound of many waters." Notice the use of the word *many*. When it comes to many waters, there is the sound of a gentle, trickling stream; the sound of a thunderstorm, with rain pouring down; the sound of waves crashing in upon the shore; and the overwhelming sound of a river at flood stage, clearing away everything in its ensuing path. God's voice today is like the sound of these many rushing waters.

This means our God is a multifaceted Creator, endlessly creative in how He chooses to communicate with each one of us. To demonstrate, let me take you to a personal page of my life's journey, when I first learned this lesson.

An Early Lesson

I have never forgotten an early lesson that impacted my spiritual life. During the Jesus Movement, I was attending a house-church-type meeting. A man from another state was ministering to us young leaders. He was a bit older than I was, and he was also more experienced in ministry.

I was sitting on the couch in the living room, minding my own business, when this man looked straight at me. He said, "Well, you feel like everything's all dried up, don't you?"

Now, at that time, I was not used to being around gifted people who had discernment, people who were capable of prophetically "reading my mail."

45

He continued, "You feel like you're not hearing God's voice right now. Is that right?"

His readout on me was sadly accurate. I had gotten used to hearing God somewhat clearly in one specific way. But often I did not know what He was saying.

The visitor continued, "It's not that God has quit speaking. It's that He has just switched channels on His dial. It's like God uses a radio when He speaks to us. God has not quit speaking to you. He has just turned the knob over to a different channel that you are not used to hearing Him on."

This man was using parabolic language; I could understand a radio changing channels. Instead of feeling condemned or exposed, I felt enlightened and encouraged. I *was* hearing God! It was just that there are many different ways the voice of God is transmitted to us. I left the room thinking, *I can't wait to discover the other ways by which my Papa God wants to speak to me!*

Our Father's voice comes to us in such a great variety of ways that we need such moments of enlightenment. Otherwise, we tend to get locked into set patterns. It is so good of God to temporarily shut down one channel in order to open up another. He has not quit speaking; He is opening our hearts and minds to hear His voice in new ways. He does this so that we will continue to grow progressively in our relationship with Him. God's goal is a real, live relationship with us.

To tell the truth, God likes messing with our radio dial! Sometimes He turns the volume louder and then back down, thus creating in us a greater dependency on Him. He loves to roll the dial to different stations to help us learn to appreciate the diversity within the Body of Christ. After we have logged a few more listening hours, we are a lot less frustrated with who controls the knobs. Eventually, we learn to love the wide variety of ways in which He speaks.

A Toolbox Full of Tools

Just as a good carpenter has more than one tool in his tool chest, so we must have a good assortment of tools available to us in order to properly build the house of the Lord. Here are a few scriptural examples that portray the diversity of tools the Spirit uses to speak to people:

1. A dream or vision (see Job 33:14–18)
2. A voice in a trance (see Acts 10:9–16)
3. The voice of many angels (see Revelation 5:11)
4. The voice of the archangel (see 1 Thessalonians 4:16)
5. The "sound of many waters" (Revelation 1:15)
6. The sound of the Lord walking in the Garden (see Genesis 3:8)
7. The sound of the army of God marching in the tops of the trees (see 2 Samuel 5:23–25)
8. The audible voice of God (see Exodus 3:4)
9. God speaking peace to His people (see Psalm 85:8)
10. God's written Word, our primary source of His voice and our chief reference point (see Psalm 119:105)
11. Wonders in the sky and on earth (see Joel 2:30–31)
12. Visions and parables given to prophets (see Hosea 12:10)
13. Words and metaphors given to prophets (see Jeremiah 18:1–6)
14. The Holy Spirit speaking to a group (see Acts 13:2)
15. Men, moved by the Holy Spirit, declaring God's voice (see 2 Peter 1:21)
16. Heavenly experiences, in which one is brought up before the Lord (see 2 Corinthians 12:1–4)
17. The Holy Spirit bearing witness to our spirit (see Romans 8:16)

18. A dumb donkey speaking with the voice of a man (see 2 Peter 2:16)
19. One person speaking the revelatory counsel of the Lord to another (see James 5:19–20)
20. God's own Son (see Hebrews 1:2)[1]

This list is not exhaustive, but it gives a bird's-eye view of some of the ways God has chosen to speak to (and through) His people. I have been surprised over the years at both how God speaks and what or whom He chooses to use. Sometimes the package is not one that I would prefer. But He *is* God—and that means He has the right to pick what He wants to say, how He wants to say it and what or whom He wants to use!

A Knowing Phone Call

One time, the voice of God came to me in the middle of the night, but I did not recognize it at first. The ringing of my telephone woke me up. I got up out of bed, went to our kitchen and picked up the phone, only to find there was no one on the other end—just a dial tone. I stumbled back into bed and fell back asleep, only to hear the phone ringing a second time. I rolled out of bed, groped in the dark and picked up the phone, only to find again that there was no voice on the other end.

Wearily, I walked back once more to my bedroom and crawled back into bed, only to be awakened a third time by hearing our telephone ringing. Determined to figure this thing out, I went to the kitchen, picked up the receiver and listened longer. I still did not hear anything. But this time, a still, small voice in my heart whispered, *Jeremiah 33:3.*

I hung up the receiver, found a Bible and looked up the verse: "Call to Me and I will answer you, and I will tell you great and mighty things, which you do not know." I was stunned by God's invitation, and I spent the next couple of hours just sitting in the quietness of our living room in the presence of the Almighty, communing with Him and listening to His sweet, sweet voice.

Now, folks, that was a genuine God encounter, a personal and unusual way for Him to demonstrate how He takes the initiative to deepen our relationship with Him. He caused the sound of a telephone to awaken me from my sleep. He persisted until He got my full attention. He took me to His written Word. His Word was illuminated by the Holy Spirit and was used to draw me closer to His very bosom. Yes, after He got my attention, I called upon the Lord, and He did show me great and mighty things that I did not previously know!

Quin Sherrer tells us:

> God speaks to us in many other ways. If we are open to hearing His voice at every turn, we will begin to recognize it with much greater frequency.[2]

Sherrer continues:

> Less dramatically, God can speak to us through an "internal witness" or a "knowing" in our innermost being, a settling peace, a conviction that the decision we might normally fret over is the right one. He can also speak through circumstances ("closed and open doors") or a seemingly serendipitous meeting that brings us an opportunity.[3]

God is not limited in His attention-getting techniques! He wants to be heard, and He has plenty of approaches He can utilize.

God's Multifaceted Voice

God does not live in a box. He did at one time, but ever since He broke out of the Ark of the Covenant, He has never lived in a box again. Of course, you and I tend to live in boxes that are often fairly nice, although cramped. They are neat but stuffy. Let's get out of the box! He wants to lift the lid over our head so that we can experience the open heavens.

Let's read Psalm 29:3–9 to get a better idea of the variety of ways we might be able to hear the voice of God:

> The voice of the LORD is upon the waters; the God of glory thunders, the LORD is over many waters. The voice of the LORD is powerful, the voice of the LORD is majestic. The voice of the LORD breaks the cedars; yes, the LORD breaks in pieces the cedars of Lebanon. He makes Lebanon skip like a calf, and Sirion like a young wild ox. The voice of the LORD hews out flames of fire. The voice of the LORD shakes the wilderness; the LORD shakes the wilderness of Kadesh. The voice of the LORD makes the deer to calve and strips the forests bare; and in His temple everything says, "Glory!"

Yes, when the powerful and glorious voice of the Lord comes into our lives, it rolls around in our spirits and "thunders" for a while (verse 3). It grabs our attention. We cannot get away from it, and we cannot get away from Him. At times, God will manifest Himself as a glorious intruder, as He did with Saul of Tarsus on the road to Damascus. If and when this occurs, we will never be the same. His voice will rock our world!

Majestic and penetrating, the voice of the Lord "breaks the cedars" (verse 5). Cedars are a very dense hardwood. (Have you ever felt someone was "too dense" for the Lord to reach?) When cedars are broken open, they release an irresistible fragrance. God's voice is capable of coming into and mowing down any situation that looms in front of us like an intimidating giant. Out of that once-foreboding giant, the aroma of Christ can come forth.

Have you ever needed to be refreshed in the Lord? Have you lost some of your zeal along the way? Need to return to your first love? Then God's voice is the cure. The intimacy of His voice will make you skip once again (see verse 6). You will feel like a child at play, ready to run, jump and leap. Your wildness will even return, and once again you will learn to love adventure.

Psalm 29 continues, "The voice of the LORD hews out flames of fire" (verse 7). Have you ever been scorched by the hot words of God? Sometimes thundering, sometimes quiet and sweet, God's voice can bring intense conviction into our lives. When His authentic fire comes, we may feel like running away from the fire rather than into it. But this fiery word and resulting experience has come to purify us for a useful purpose. Let the fire fall, and let His word purify, cleanse and burn out all of the dross and impurities within your heart.

Moving on to verse 8, we find that the "voice of the LORD shakes the wilderness." In truth, this can be pretty uncomfortable. God shakes everything that can be shaken so that that which cannot be shaken will remain. I don't want my life to be built on a foundation that cannot hold up under such pressure. The voice of the Lord will try the foundations of our lives. God makes sure our lives are built upon the solid rock of Jesus Christ and His righteousness. During times of trial, pressure and shaking, we need to let those difficulties propel us to become unshakable.

Do you want creativity to abound in your life? Tired of your own ideas and formulas? Then listen for the voice of the Lord, because it makes the "deer to calve" (verse 9). The voice of the Lord creates faith in the hearer. It changes your circumstances from barren to fruitful.

I know this from experience. My wife and I were diagnosed as medically barren. But the word of the Lord came forth, and faith was conceived—and so were four children! We know the voice of the Lord causes the deer to calve. So, know this: It is never too late for fresh life to emerge. Dormant dreams become activated in a moment by the voice of God. May His word come upon you and cause you to see yourself as a fruitful vine. "And [the voice of the Lord] strips the forests bare" (verse 9). How do you like that one? God's voice comes, and it removes all the false armor that we rely on. All of our vanities, self-reliance, false images and pretenses are stripped away, and we are left naked before the Creator of the universe. The voice of God brings humility into our lives. According to John 15, it is the tree that has borne fruit that He prunes. So let's be encouraged, looking at the end result and remembering how good He is. If He strips us or asks us to lay something down, He always has a great reason.

God wants us to hear His voice not just yesterday but also today and in a vibrant relationship, with all of its manifestations, so that we can bear much fruit—fruit that will remain.

The End Result

In our process of becoming, we must not forget that, ultimately, this is not about us. It is about our being transformed into the beautiful image of God's glorious Son, Jesus. By the power of the sound of many waters, which is our personal guide and tutor, the Holy Spirit, you and I will be changed into the image of God's Son. We will shout praises together as we are changed from glory to glory. Everything in God's temple says, "Glory!"

So let His voice thunder. Let the fire fall. Let His word be magnified. Let the waterfall of His refreshing sound replenish each and every thing. Let all creation echo His sound. Let His still, small voice and His tumultuous voice continue to proceed from the throne of God into your life.

Remember, you and I do not live by bread alone but by the ever-proceeding word of our Father. This is what gave me life in the past. It is how I live today. And it is how I will live my life in the future: by hearing God's voice.

Yes, everything in His temple shouts "Glory!" Come on, now. Do it with me. Give Him some praise, and watch what the Lord will do!

Lord, let Your voice be like the sound of many rushing waters in my life. Impart dreams and visions and an increase of the spirit of wisdom and revelation to me. Release Your angelic hosts to minister unto me and my family. Open up Your written Word by that same spirit of wisdom and revelation. Turn the logos—*the written* Word—*into a revelatory spoken word in my life. Open up new expressions of Your voice to me today. Amen and amen!*

THINK ABOUT IT

1. See if you can list five different ways God's voice came to you this very week. (Think about everything that happened. Do you remember a bit of a dream? Did a verse from the Bible jump off the page at you? Did you experience deep peace? Did your spirit say *amen* to one of the points in your pastor's sermon? Did a friend call to encourage you?)

2. Take some time right now to worship God. Expect Him to draw near to you as you do so.

4

Walking in Our Kingdom Birthright

But you are a chosen race, a royal priesthood, a holy nation, a people for God's own possession, so that you may proclaim the excellencies of Him who has called you out of darkness into His marvelous light.

1 Peter 2:9

And He has made us to be a kingdom, priests to His God and Father—to Him be the glory and the dominion forever and ever. Amen.

Revelation 1:6

For all who are being led by the Spirit of God, these are sons of God.

Romans 8:14

If we live by the Spirit, let us also walk by the Spirit.

Galatians 5:25

Everyone who is a born-again believer in the Lord Jesus Christ has been translated from the kingdom of darkness into the Kingdom of light. We are citizens of a new nation, a holy nation. We are priests in this new Kingdom, and we have the privilege of ministering to God Himself. Whether we are Asian, Russian, Mexican, African, French, Spanish, British, Chinese, Indian, German, American, Canadian or any other nationality by natural birth, by supernatural birth we are members of the best family, the best bloodline and the best race on the planet. You and I are God's own possession, members of a chosen race!

Just as we have rights, privileges and responsibilities that come with our natural citizenship, so do we have the same in the spiritual realm. As citizens of the Kingdom of God, we have rights, privileges and responsibilities concerning the King of kings and Lord of lords.

A Priest and a Prophet

As full citizens and members of this royal priesthood of the Lord, we have the right to request, at any time, a personal audience with the Master of the universe. We can come boldly before His throne of grace to bring our requests. As priests, we represent our nations, our neighborhoods, our families and our friends before the throne of almighty God. We can cast our cares upon the Lord, make intercession on behalf of others or simply come to commune with the lover of our soul.

Just as we have the right as Kingdom citizens to make our appeals before the King, the King has the right to issue commands, decrees, desires and orders to His people. He is more eager than most people realize to exercise His sovereignty, especially when

He speaks from heaven to invade our comfort zones—although we can misinterpret His intentions. Sometimes even the idea that God speaks is too much for us to handle.

In *Surprised by the Power of the Spirit*, Jack Deere writes about how his personal paradigm shifted regarding this. He says that the most difficult transition from his old kind of Christianity to a new and improved one was not learning to accept that God heals and does miracles today. Rather, the thing that took the most convincing, that he resisted the most and that he was most afraid of, was accepting that God still *speaks* today.[1]

Yes, God still speaks today, and He has the authority to speak to whomever He wants whenever He wants and however He wants. As citizens of this Kingdom, we need to know that He wants to speak to us and that it is part of our birthright to be able to hear His voice—not just yesterday, but today.

The thing is, God's ways are not our ways. Even when we accept that He wants to communicate with us, we have a long-term learning process ahead of us. We have some unlearning as well as some new learning to do.

Baby Steps

Before a child runs, he or she walks. Before walking comes toddling. And before toddling—I can attest to this, having been a young father of four children and now as a grandfather to a growing number of grandchildren—comes *falling*. Babies, holding on to anything they can, launch out over and over, then topple or trip down to the floor. Each of us started this way. The amazing thing is how kids just get up and try to walk again. Babies don't see this falling business as discouraging. The goal—walking—is way too enticing to let a few troubles be a deterrent.

Likewise, no one has a perfect start as he or she learns the Kingdom walk. We all learn by trial and error. However, persistence will be rewarded.

We *will* fall. I cannot recount how many times I thought I heard God, only to find out later that I had missed something important. Of course, I can also look back at some of those times when I thought I must have heard Him incorrectly, only to find out later that I really *had* heard Him correctly after all. It is all part of the learning process.

Today, some people acknowledge me as an international prophet and a global prayer leader. But before I became that kind of person, I had to take many baby steps.

One such baby step occurred in one of our Jesus People meetings. I thought I was receiving a word from God, so I launched out to make it public. The worship had come to a hush; it seemed like the appropriate moment. All ears were directed my way as I blurted, "Out of your innermost being shall come forth *livers* of living water!" The place erupted into laughter. I wanted to find an escape hatch in the floor somewhere so that I could quickly slip out of view. I corrected myself—"I mean *rivers!*"—but it was too late. The *livers* were already out on the table for all to see, never to be stuffed down again. I really don't recall how the rest of the meeting went. I guess the teacher taught something and the meeting came to a close. But, oh, how I wanted to just go home!

When I did go back to the Jesus House, where some of us Jesus People young men lived, I went to His Word. I found this in Proverbs 24:16: "For a righteous man falls seven times, and rises again." I decided God's people are not quitters, so neither was I. On my next time out of the stalls, I knew that a bunch of hurdles, such as the fear of man and the fear of rejection, would be standing right in front of me. By the grace of God, I continued to use His gift and respond to His call to convey

His heart to people, in spite of a few more bleeps and blunders and escapades. Through my mistakes, I learned to hear God's voice and release His revelation more accurately and effectively.

We all must learn lessons of humility, swallow some pride, seek the Lord for strength and wisdom and move on from past mistakes. The important thing is to *keep moving on*. Making mistakes is not unpardonable. We all have made them, and we all will make them in the future. We must learn from our mistakes. We need to turn them over to our Master and let Him use them for His own glory. We can depend on it: All things *do* work together for the good of those who keep on loving God (see Romans 8:28), in spite of temporary setbacks.

It is not always an easy walk or even an easy learning curve. It can be very difficult to find out that we are wrong, especially when we really think we have heard God's voice. Only the Lord's mercy and goodness keep us going, as progress comes by trial and error. It is a relationship with God, not just a set of skills, that we are growing in.

If we persistently engage the Lord and His will with our whole heart, we will become proficient in not only hearing but also discerning His voice. This is His desire for us, our birthright, the Kingdom walk into which we have been invited. It happens one step at a time.

A Few More Steps

Besides being willing to mess up and pull ourselves back up whenever we fall, how do we grow in our ability to hear from God? The simplest answer to this question is this: He teaches us, one step at a time!

One of my neighbors, who is also a friend of many years, teaches about hearing God's voice by reminding us of how children grow. When we are young in the Lord, our Papa is there to speak to us in ways we can easily understand. Like young children, when we begin to follow Him, we need the directions spelled out for us. To hear those directions, my friend says that each of us has a sweet spot in our heart that is important to the process. The Holy Spirit knows where that sweet spot is and how to touch it, and He speaks right to it. We melt; we swoon—we are in love. God talks; we hear; we respond. We are on a honeymoon with Jesus, and it is great!

Then, before we know it, we reduce what God has said into pat equations. But to keep us in a fresh love relationship with God, it seems as if God changes the rules without telling us. We are no longer "babes in Toyland." It can seem that God is no longer speaking at all, or at least that He is not speaking in a way we can understand. We know He loves us. We know He is there—at least, we think He is. But the heavens are brass, and it seems that our Papa just is not interested in us anymore. At those times, we think He has gone on vacation or out to lunch. We are tempted to feel, *He used to know my address, but either I moved, He moved or He lost it somewhere!* I call this "When God Seems Silent" or "When the Lollipop Ends."

The truth of the situation is that God is making sure we grow up. Gifts of grace are given in the wet, rainy seasons of life, but the personal character traits we need in order to carry the gifts are forged in the testing of the desert times. God knows we need both.

By the way, even when we get older in God, those sweet spots in our heart are still there. When He touches one of those areas, we weep, we become a puddle, and we are captured once again. He knows how to reel us into His heart.

Papa God speaks to us at our present level while at the same time always prodding us to move on, to grow and to mature. Our Father wants us to reach higher levels. To do so, we cannot keep communicating at our familiar level. We cannot forever be talking baby talk, so to speak.

We must make another shift, go through another time of growth and take another lesson in His language of love. We must embrace another opportunity to exercise faith in the reality that He is with us whether we feel His presence or not. He has promised never to leave us or forsake us, and we can take that one to the bank any day of the week.

I love to feel His presence, but my faith in Him is not based on how much I feel. It is based on His Word of promise. His name is Emmanuel, meaning "God with us."

God's loving desire to be in communication with us never ebbs or ceases. We will soon find out that we are the ones who need to change. We are the ones who must lean into His heart to hear His sweet love language. As Paul teaches us, "When I was a child, I used to speak as a child, think as a child, reason like a child; when I became a man, I did away with childish things" (1 Corinthians 13:11).

Speak Less, Listen More

We cannot leapfrog down the road the fast way; rather, learning to hear God takes time. Hearing God takes patience, too. If we don't realize this, we won't set aside enough time to listen, to seek Him or to inquire of Him. Our Western society does not teach us the art of listening. But the connection is obvious: If we want to hear, we must listen. I recommend speaking a little less and listening a whole lot more. Here is another hint: If we don't make time, He will help us to make time. He knows how to get our attention.

My personal tutor, the Holy Spirit, has taught me many lessons about this. For example, over the years, I have been awakened in the middle of the night hundreds, if not thousands, of times. At first, I did not understand what was going on. I tried (unsuccessfully) to turn over in bed and go back to sleep. I rebuked sleep disorders: "Get out of here, in Jesus' name!" But it did not work. It took a while to figure out what He wanted me to do, which was to wait and watch with Him for a while, after which I could do what I wanted to do—sleep!

Over a period of time, I learned to get up out of bed (highly important—get *out* of the bed!) in the middle of the night and go sit in my recliner chair in our living room. I did not do a lot of heavy intercession or spiritual burden-bearing. I was just there. For a while, I thought I was wasting both God's time and my own. But eventually I learned the lesson: All He wanted was me. He simply wanted a friend, a companion and a lover with whom He could share His heart. I have learned more about God's voice in the wee hours of the morning than at any other time. Now I love being "on call" to be with Him. It is a privilege to be called and chosen to be His friend.

During the quiet hours of the night, I have learned to turn the ear of my spirit in His direction. One of the most common ways I hear from the Lord is simply by hearing the quiet inner voice of the Holy Spirit. God can and does speak to me in many ways, but He comes to me most often through His peaceful inner voice, which communes with my heart.

As a mother trains her ear to hear her babe, even when she is asleep, we need to train our ears to hear the slightest whisper from God. It will take time and repetition, but with the help of the Holy Spirit, who really is our private, personal tutor, we can learn how to pay attention. We need to make the effort, take the time and set aside portions of our days or nights. He greatly desires to help us and empower us.

Hearing God's voice will not happen automatically. If we take time to be with Him, we will hear what the Lord our God is speaking. I guarantee it.

Ready for a Revolution

About forty years ago, a new sound broke forth from England, and it quickly swept the world. A singing group called the Beatles took the nations by storm. Their simple, catchy lyrics captured hearts and promoted change. One of their top songs was "Revolution." It helped throw an impressionable generation into a wild frenzy of drugs, free love and rebellion against authority.

Forty years later, another new sound can be heard. Another generation of people is discontented with the status quo. A radical yet intimate sound of prayer and worship is invading the Church and beginning to make a worldwide impact. I believe we are on the verge of a societal prophetic revolution—a dramatic shift. Watch out, world; watch out, slumbering Church! This sleepy Bride is about to shake off her passivity and arise and become all that God has destined her to be. A clarion call to change and intimacy is ringing across the land. Draft notices are being sent out from heaven: Wanted—Passionate, Consecrated Warriors.[2]

Great change is coming. But first, great change must come to us in our own personal walks with God. When this happens—if and only when this happens—then great change will suddenly appear in the global Body of Christ. My heart echoes the cries of Michael Brown, theologian and founder of the FIRE School of Ministry on the East Coast of the United States. In his radical book *Revolution! The Call to Holy War*, he declares:

> Why is this dedication to a cause—this passionate, often selfless, sometimes murderous, always fanatical dedication—characteristic of revolutionary movements? It is because the revolutionary has an unshakable conviction that something is terribly wrong with society, that something very important is missing, that something major needs to change, indeed, that it must change now.[3]

Sam Storms, teacher, author and former faculty member of Wheaton College, trumpets similar thoughts in his book *The Beginner's Guide to Spiritual Gifts*:

> I want you to be expectant about what God can do for you and for those he's called you to help with his power. I want your faith and confidence in both God's goodness and his greatness to grow and intensify. Skeptics about what God can do will rarely experience his power.[4]

Let's dare to believe that when we ask for directions, we will receive them. Let's start by changing our expectations and looking for the blueprints that God wants to release. Let's believe that the Holy Spirit is our personal tutor and that He has plans for our lives. Let's believe that we have a Kingdom birthright to hear from God. Let's believe that God actually does hear our prayers!

Are you beginning to be a believing believer? Are you engaging your spirit to expect to receive revelation from God? Before you know it, you will be hearing His present-day voice in your life and you will be passing on this contagious passion to others. When this happens, there will be a revolution in the Church. It is our destiny. It is our Kingdom birthright. So let's walk in our inheritance, for Jesus Christ's sake!

Father God, I declare that, in Christ, I am a citizen of another realm. I have a Kingdom birthright and Kingdom privileges. I choose not to despise the day of a small beginning. I choose to walk in the light of Your Word and ways. I am ready for more lessons in the School of the Spirit. I want to be a part of a true revolution in the earth. Praise the Lord! Amen!

THINK ABOUT IT

1. Have you ever said, "Help! I've fallen, and I can't get up"? Turn those words into a prayer:

   Help, Lord. I've fallen, and I need Your help to get back up.

2. Earlier in your Christian walk, were you able to hear God's voice more than you do now? How can you respond to His invitation to listen for His words?

5

Built upon the Rock

Thy Word is a lamp to my feet, and a light unto
my path.

Psalm 119:105 KJV

"Everyone who comes to Me and hears My words
and acts on them, I will show you whom he is like:
he is like a man building a house, who dug deep
and laid a foundation on the rock; and when a flood
occurred, the torrent burst against that house and
could not shake it, because it had been well built.
But the one who has heard and has not acted ac-
cordingly, is like a man who built a house on the
ground without any foundation; and the torrent
burst against it and immediately it collapsed, and
the ruin of that house was great."

Luke 6:47–49

> Be diligent to present yourself approved to God as
> a workman who does not need to be ashamed, ac-
> curately handling the word of truth.
>
> 2 Timothy 2:15

> Let the word of Christ dwell in you richly.
>
> Colossians 3:16 NKJV

I have traveled thousands of miles in recent years, crisscross-
ing many nations by airplane, train and automobile. Scores
of times, what has helped me get to the right place at the right
time is a good road map, either printed or electronic. Turning
on my cell phone to check in with the right person at the last
minute has saved my neck more than once. Though I am sensi-
tive in my spiritual orientation, I tend naturally to be one who
gets lost rather easily.

Those who know me well call me directionally challenged.
I need all the help I can get! It is totally true that I need a GPS
system to navigate properly. I need a Global Prayer Storm behind
me. I need God's Presence System.

Thankfully, God has not left us on our own, mapless or help-
less, to try to figure out how to get to His destinations. He has
given us our personal tutor, the Holy Spirit, to guide us into all
truth. He has also given us His road map of life, the Word of
God. This manual spells out in plain print much of our most
desperately needed direction. But as with any road map, it won't
do us much good if we keep it stuffed away in our glove box
or on a shelf, collecting dust. We have to take it out and use it.

If we have not read our Bible, we should not act like we
know where we are going. Without it, we could take a wrong
turn on the road and double the length of time it takes to get
to our destination. We need to get smart! We need to take out

the map and study it so that we get to know the territory we are entering. We need to review the road map many times, in order to end up at the right place without running out of gas or even running off the road.

To complete our journey with the Lord, we must study, read and meditate on the written Word of God. As we read it and chew on it, His Word will begin to dwell richly in our hearts and minds, and we will reach the destination He has planned for our lives.

Know Your Companion and Friend

Like most pastors, I own several editions of the greatest Book ever written. But there is one that has been my daily companion for more than twenty years. It is torn; it falls apart often; it has been around the world with me. My favorite Bible is marked full of love notes from my kids, such as the one our third child, Tyler, gave to me when he was about three years old. Innocently, he tore Isaiah 42 and 43 to shreds. My wife quickly gathered up the fragments of those favorite chapters of mine, taped the little pieces all back together and, before I got home, stuck them back in my Bible where they belonged. They are still that way today—and I love it! A bit later, little Rachel, our fourth child, decided to draw pictures for me in 1 Peter in red ink. Her scribbles are there today, and I love every blot!

Once while I was on staff with Metro Christian Fellowship in Kansas City, I was in one of the upstairs offices doing some prayer counseling. I always took my favorite Bible with me, just in case I needed to give a Scripture to someone as a bit of medicine for what might be ailing him or her. But after that appointment, I could not find my favorite brown leather New American Standard Bible for days, so I used other Bibles. They were okay. But I felt a bit lost. My personal Bible contained sermon notes I had written when I had heard the teachings of Mike Bickle, Francis Frangipane, Jack Deere, Mahesh Chavda and many others. *Where did my Bible go?*, I kept asking myself. I cried out to the Lord, *Where is my Bible?*

For many days, I used what I call the Necessary in Vineyard Bible—the New International Version. I chomped on the New King James. I tried huffing down the original King James Version. All of these are great versions, but I did not feel right without my familiar version.

After about four weeks of this, I wandered back upstairs in the Metro office building to the same room where I had had my appointment. There was my brown leather Bible, lying on the carpet. I gleefully exclaimed, "I found my friend! I found my lost friend!"

I was beside myself with joy. I felt the Holy Spirit was pleased that I was so pleased. It is the Word of God—so much more than a book of doctrine, history or good teaching—and it just did not taste the same if I wasn't chewing on my favorite copy. I had been lost, as if someone had switched road signs on me.

I now have grown used to using online versions and even Bible apps. But the real issue is: Are you storing up the Word of God in your life? Do you have a "close friend" Bible, one with words you can hide in your heart readily, one you can chew on? I read my favorite Bible—and it reads me! It is the only book ever written that is not just ink on a page; it is alive and active, sharper than any two-edged sword (see Hebrews 4:12).

Store Up the Word of God

We are admonished to hide God's Word in our heart (see Psalm 119:11). As we do this consistently, we establish safety, security and protection for our lives. We then have a basis from which to judge the multitude of voices that come our way. We have a vast well of His words to draw from in times of need.

There is a direct correlation between *hearing* and *hiding* the Word of God within our heart and mind. Both of these activities involve action. To the degree we actively hide the Word of God in our soul, we can expect to hear the revelatory, or spoken, word of God resounding in our heart. Hiding and hearing are divinely connected!

I grew up in a rural community, where my mother was famous for her canned produce, which she had grown in our large garden. She would often put up a hundred quarts of green beans and dozens of pints of corn, homemade pickles and even bottles of grape juice. In the heat of the Midwest summer, she would get out her pressure cooker in our little kitchen to produce food that would feed her family during the winter ahead. When winter set in, we were glad that Mom had invested so much time storing up in a time of plenty for a time of need.

Just as my mother stored up fruit, vegetables and produce to be used, eaten and enjoyed at a later date, so we are to store up the written Word of God (*logos* in Greek) so it later can be "eaten" as a life-producing spoken word (*rhema* in Greek). Through reading, studying, repeating, memorizing, praying and meditating on the written Word, we accumulate an enormous resource in our mind and heart that can be submitted to the Holy Spirit's transforming power. A quickening work of God occurs, and the written *logos* becomes activated into a present-tense, spoken, *rhema* word of God.

The term *logos* (written word) is used 331 times in the Greek New Testament. The word *rhema* (spoken word) is used more than seventy times in the New Testament. *Logos* is used well over four times as often as is *rhema*, which helps us to see the relative importance of the *logos*, the sure foundation, the written Word of God.

Vine's Expository Dictionary of New Testament Words states:

> The significance of rhema as distinct from logos is exemplified in the injunction to take up the sword of the Spirit which is the Word of God, or the spoken rhema word used in Ephesians 6:17. Here the reference is not to the whole Bible as such but to an individual Scripture, which the spirit brings to our remembrance for our use in a time of need, a prerequisite being the regular storing of the mind with the Scripture.[1]

Below are some further differentiations that show the relationship between the written Word of God and the spoken word:

1. *Planning and execution. Logos* is that which is in the mind before communication occurs. *Rhema* is the vocalization, the articulation involved in expression. *Logos* is the thinking, and *rhema* is the saying. *Logos* signifies the thought, and *rhema* emphasizes the speaking.

2. *Message and vehicle. Logos* connotes the planning and the purpose. *Rhema* represents the execution of the plan or its oral expression. *Logos* is the content; rhema is the vehicle for the context. *Rhema* emphasizes a spoken message or the preached Gospel, while *logos* stresses the message itself.

3. *Whole and part. Logos* can signify the whole speech, the entire message or the complete doctrine. *Rhema* can represent the individual supporting arguments. *Logos* tends toward the whole, while *rhema* means a specific part of the total word.

If we want to move in the inspirational *rhema* element of the Word, we must store up the *logos* content of the Word. We can't have one without the other!

Hear the Word to Release Faith

We read many things, but do we always really hear what we read? Romans 10:17 tells us, "Faith comes from hearing [*acoa* in Greek], and hearing by the word [*rhema*] of Christ." *Acoa* means "to have audience with, to come with ears."

This is vitally important. The inner attitude of our heart will determine whether we have heard what is being stated. In other words, we can read the written Word and leave unchanged. But if we approach the Word of God with the correct inner attitude of the heart, by coming with ears ready to listen, we will give full attention to the Word, have an audience with it and leave changed. If we come with a heart of submission, expecting to receive, like a child or student expects to receive from his or her caring parent or teacher, we will receive much.

How do we develop these important inner attitudes and expectancies that will determine how we hear and thus what we receive? Glancing again at Romans 10:17—"Faith comes from hearing"—we see that our faith comes and continues to come by having an ongoing audience with God's words through the fellowship of the Holy Spirit.

Our faith quickens us, energizes us, releases us and motivates us to take action. It requires the written Word and the spoken word, the *logos* and the *rhema*, to be brought together by the Spirit of God, who activates and releases the effect of God's Word, creating faith in our lives.

I want to receive and exercise faith. I know that faith pleases God. It enables me to live in new life. So, if I want to hear God's voice, I must come to God with my ears on. Will you do the same?

Meditate on the Word of Life

We can read the Word. We can pray based on the words we read. But the approach to the Scriptures that will best help us to turn the *logos* into *rhema* is the spiritual discipline of *meditating* on the Word of Life.

In my book *The Lost Art of Practicing His Presence*, I attempted to dust off the art of Christian meditation and give some clarity to it. I wrote that the word *meditate* means "to think deeply or to reflect on something." To *reflect* on something means "to contemplate or ponder it." *Contemplate* means "to gaze at or think about intensely."[2]

These words are slow, careful words. When we are meditating on Scripture, it is not so much the amount of text we read as what we chew. It may be no more than a single verse. It may only be a few words, such as, "As the deer pants for the water" (Psalm 42:1). Peter Toon, author of *Meditating as a Christian*, writes, "Meditation is . . . taking to heart, reading slowly and carefully, prayerfully taking in, and humbly receiving into mind, heart, and will that which God has revealed . . . by the indwelling Spirit of Christ."[3]

I often turn to the contemporary writings of Richard Foster, a brilliant author and writer on the spiritual disciplines. In *Prayer: Finding the Heart's True Home*, he writes:

> In Meditative Prayer the Bible ceases to be a quotation dictionary and becomes instead "wonderful words of life" that lead us to the Word of Life. It differs even from the study of Scripture. Whereas the study of Scripture centers on exegesis, the meditation upon Scripture centers on internalizing and personalizing the passage. The written Word becomes a living word addressed to us.[4]

Meditation is an awesome tool to aid all of us as believers in hearing the voice of God. Let's chew on the Word of God. It is our daily bread.

Gathering Manna

The children of Israel had manna as their daily bread when they wandered in the wilderness. It was bread from heaven:

> Then the LORD said to Moses, "Behold, I will rain bread from heaven for you; and the people shall go out and gather a day's portion every day, that I may test them, whether or not they will walk in My instruction. On the sixth day, when they prepare what they bring in, it will be twice as much as they gather daily." . . .
>
> In the morning there was a layer of dew around the camp. When the layer of dew evaporated, behold, on the surface of the wilderness there was a fine flake-like thing, fine as the frost on the ground. When the sons of Israel saw it, they said to one another, "What is it?" For they did not know what it was. And Moses said to them, "It is the bread which the LORD has given you to eat."
>
> Exodus 16:4–5, 13–15

The Israelites did not know what the flake-like things were. Many times God's voice or even provision comes in a way that we do not instantly identify as such. We do not readily recognize the answers to our very own prayers. We respond, "What is this? That can't be God!"

The story continues in verses 16–19:

> "This is what the LORD has commanded, 'Gather of it every man as much as he should eat; you shall take an omer apiece according to the number of persons each of you has in his tent.'" The sons of Israel did so, and some gathered much and some little. . . . He who had gathered much had no excess, and he who had gathered little had no lack; every man gathered as much as he should eat. Moses said to them, "Let no man leave any of it until morning."

But some did not follow Moses' orders, and they left part of it until the next day, and it bred worms. When the Israelites obeyed the Lord's commandments, every family had all that they needed. When they obeyed, the manna did not spoil.

Applying Manna to Real Life

We must gather the Word as manna every day. Our portion today is only good for today. We cannot live off yesterday's manna. If we do not eat today's portion, we will have lack and need. But if we abide in His Word daily, we will have life within. That is the basic message here. We cannot live life today on yesterday's Word. By the same token, we cannot expect to hear God's *rhema* today when we haven't gathered in His *logos* yesterday or last week or last month, chewing it and digesting it. We cannot get God's voice activated in our life today without first putting it into our heart and mind.

It's an issue of obedience. Each of us needs to gather his or her own manna, although we may gather and eat it together, in each other's company.

Once I was praying for someone, and I was about to jump in and solve his problem for him. Suddenly, it was as if the Holy Spirit slapped my hand and said to me, *Don't put the spoon in his mouth! Put it in his hand, and teach him how to feed himself.* We must equip and teach each other the necessities of the spiritual disciplines, such as reading and meditating on Scripture. There is no substitute!

If we want to end up at the right place at the right time to see the written Word turn into an immediate word from God, if we want faith that pleases God and if we want to hear His sweet voice, get out a road map, read it and follow the directions. We will surely make it to the end of our journey with manna to spare, just as the Israelites experienced every Sabbath, when the extra food they had gathered did not spoil as it did on the other days.

The Word of God is your road map for the journey of life. If we are to be built upon the rock, then we must return to the one true and strong foundation, God's Word. And the One who wrote it, the Holy Spirit, is your personal tutor, waiting to speak a word into your ear: "This is the way, walk in it" (Isaiah 30:21).

Father God, by the grace You supply, my life shall be built upon the rock of Your Word. I love the Word of God. The Bible is full of words of life for me. Teach me how to meditate upon and digest more of the amazing Word of God. I declare that I am growing in faith as I store up Your Word in my heart. I will hear what the Spirit is saying to me through the written Word. For Jesus Christ's sake, Amen.

THINK ABOUT IT

1. Why does God's spoken word depend on His written Word? In your personal experience, can you point to a time when you may have bypassed this connection?

2. Do you take time every day to gather manna from Scripture? What can you do to grow in your relationship with the Word of God so your life can be built upon the rock?

6

Ten Practical, Personal Tools

"Therefore everyone who hears these words of Mine and acts on them, may be compared to a wise man who built his house on the rock. And the rain fell, and the floods came, and the winds blew and slammed against that house; and yet it did not fall, for it had been founded on the rock."

Matthew 7:24–25

Trust in the LORD with all your heart and do not lean on your own understanding. In all your ways acknowledge Him, and He will make your paths straight.

Proverbs 3:5–6

The Holy Spirit is called the finger of God. The finger points the way. The finger helps to personally identify who is who. The finger releases a touch of tenderness. At the tip of a finger, there is a distinct design called the fingerprint. To effectively hear the voice of God today, we need the practical and personal work of the Holy Spirit.

Thus far, we have been laying a firm foundation for our house of God to be built upon. It is time now to learn from Jesus, our Master Carpenter, how to use a few tools—ten of them, actually—that can assist us in the art of hearing and following God's voice today. It is time for us to be practical and pragmatic.[1] So let me give you some relatable and applicable points.

1. Don't Make It Complicated

It is not hard to hear God. We tend to overcomplicate the whole matter. The following three simple steps will help us hear God's gracious voice.

Step 1: Submit to His lordship.

Let's ask God to help silence our thoughts, desires and opinions. We want to hear only the thoughts of the Lord. Take the advice that is given in Proverbs 3:6–7: "In all your ways acknowledge Him, and He will make your paths straight. Do not be wise in your own eyes; fear the LORD and turn away from evil."

George Müller, an Englishman who was one of the great evangelical champions of the faith, lived this first principle. By faith alone, he supported vast orphanages. He would pray daily for the provisions to feed the hundreds of children who were under his care. One of the secrets in George Müller's walk with God was so simple, yet it is rarely taught today: He told his followers that if they wanted to hear from God and pray in faith, then they first would have to cleanse themselves of their own opinions. Another word for this is *submission.*

We cannot hear God if we have a preformed opinion on an issue. We must submit to His lordship. We need to consciously submit our thoughts, our opinions, our preconceived attitudes and notions and even our traditions to the Lord.

Step 2: Resist the enemy.

We can use the authority Jesus Christ has given us as His disciples to silence the voice of the enemy. We can stand firm in our position as God's own children. We need to learn what it means to apply the blood of Jesus over our lives. We can resist the enemy, who comes to our mind with all sorts of fears and plausible doubts. God's Spirit in us will make us able to do what we can never do solo, and Jesus' powerful name will convince Satan to leave.

The apostle James wrote, "Submit therefore to God. Resist the devil and he will flee from you" (James 4:7). Submit first; then resist.

Step 3: Ask a question and expect God's answer.

We should ask the very question that is in our heart, bringing it before the throne of almighty God. Then we need to wait for Him to answer. We should not expect an answer to pop right up ("You've got mail!"); rather, we should wait expectantly, believing that as we have submitted to God and resisted the enemy, we will be "filled with the knowledge of His will in all spiritual wisdom and understanding" (Colossians 1:9). At times, an immediate reply may come. This vital third step after submitting and resisting is to *expect* God to act. When God acts, we all win!

2. Allow God to Speak How He Chooses

We should not try to dictate to God the guidance methods we prefer; rather, we must listen with a yielded heart. There is a direct link between yielding and hearing. He may choose to speak to us in a method that we are not accustomed to. He can speak through His written Word, through a person, through dreams or visions or through a quiet inner voice.

Having submitted to Him, resisted the enemy and asked for an answer, we should not dictate the way we want God to respond to our request. Let's receive grace from His storehouse—the grace of expectant yielding. We need to always allow God to speak in the way He chooses.

3. Confess Any Known Sins

A clean heart is a prerequisite to hearing God. We read in Psalm 66:18, "If I regard wickedness in my heart, the Lord will not hear." If the Lord doesn't even hear us, then we are not going to receive the answer that we are hoping for—because He hasn't even heard us ask the question.

This tool for hearing God's voice is foundational to the ABCs of Christianity—the confession of sins. We need to confess our sins to our Father in Jesus' great name. He is waiting to forgive us.

4. Obey the Last Thing God Said

Why would God give us new orders if we have not obeyed His last ones? He is waiting for us to do what He has already told us to do. This alone could be a primary roadblock for hearing God's voice today. If He has already spoken and we already know what is required of us, then we should go do it—for Jesus' sake! It is an issue of obedience.

These principles are laid out in the story about Elisha the prophet and the servant who was rigorously chopping down some trees with which to expand the place where they were living:

So he went . . . to the Jordan, [and] they cut down trees. But as one was felling a beam, the axe head fell into the water; and he cried out and said, "Alas, my master! For it was borrowed." Then the man of God said, "Where did it fall?" And when he showed him the place, he cut off a stick and threw it in there, and made the iron float. He said, "Take it up for yourself." So he put out his hand and took it.

2 Kings 6:4–7

Here is the Goll paraphrase:

The servant has been working away, cutting down trees with his axe. It seems that all of a sudden, he flies off the handle—oops, I mean the axe head does! Things got dull, and he lost his cutting edge. The servant temporarily stopped tending to his relationship with the head of the axe.

Now, here is the reality: An axe head does not become loosened up all at once. This occurs over time, due to neglect. When the cutting edge is not sharpened after the axe is used for a job, the cutting edge grows dull. Eventually, the woodcutter needs to put more of his strength into every swing. He still gets results, but each time, a little more of his strength is needed and a little duller edge is formed on the axe. Over time, the axe head becomes terribly dull. It loses its tight fit with the handle. When it eventually falls off the handle, this seems to happen all of a sudden, but, really, we know better.

If it can happen that way in the natural, it also can happen that way in the spiritual. We need to tend to our axe head, keeping it sharp. We should make sure that our relationship is right with the Head of the Body of Christ. We should not wait six months before asking the Holy Spirit to turn on His lights inside for an inspection; rather, we need to do that every day! Make it practical and make it personal.

In my own relationship with the Holy Spirit, I often sanctify three days of fasting just for the purpose of cleansing my heart. I am not asking God for stuff; I am asking God to tenderize my heart. Knowing that I still sin and realizing that sin makes me lose my edge and that it loosens my connection with the Lord, I need to take a maintenance break. Like anyone else, I can end up putting too much of my own strength into situations, and, as a result, my head can get lost in the field of my labors. I may even fly off the handle. Then (good news!), the Son of God comes along and says to me, "Ah, I see you lost your head. You flew off the handle, eh? Where did it fall?" And when I show Him the exact place, my cutting edge will be summoned. It is as much of a miracle as an iron axe head that floats—I am restored, complete and useful.

What is the key for receiving back the cutting edge? We must point out the place where we lost it. We must go back to the place where we heard and have not yet obeyed. As both James and Peter write, "God is opposed to the proud, but gives grace to the humble" (James 4:6; 1 Peter 5:5). The condition for grace has just been met.

When, in humility, we point out our place of falling, Jesus takes a stick (a symbol of the cross), then throws the wood of His own cross into the place of our failure, and a miracle happens! We don't have to conjure up some religious performance; the voice of God is back. We have been restored. He is within us. The axe head surfaces and comes back to the shore on the waves, to be restored to its proper place of usefulness.

5. Tune In to God's Voice

God will use others to confirm our guidance, but we must learn to hear the voice of the Lord for ourselves. God is a jealous God. That means He wants to talk with us personally. We need to become secure in our own identity in Christ. We must realize that we are sons and daughters of the Creator of the universe and that He wants to relate to us in our own right.

We should not be wrongly codependent on others. At the same time, we should not jump the tracks by cultivating an independent and rebellious spirit. We need to hear God for ourselves while honoring the body of Christ.

6. Don't Talk About It Too Soon

In all truth, I wish I had known about this tool a bit earlier in my life. I think the dreamer Joseph might have wished he had heard this one, too! Waiting to speak the words God has given us helps us avoid not-so-obvious pitfalls. When God tells us something, it is as if He is sharing a secret with a trusted friend. We should consider asking permission to speak it out loud before opening wide our mouth and repeating everything we supposedly know.

Here are four traps I have discovered with speaking God's words too soon:

The Trap of Pride

Just because we have heard the Lord does not mean that we have developed the character to carry out the action. We might think, *Man, am I a hotshot! I heard God today.* We center more around ourselves and our gifts instead of the Master and His ways, becoming prideful.

The Trap of Presumption

Presumption makes us act as if we know it all. After all, we have heard God! Could it be that we heard only part of what God wanted to say? One portion could be coming through some life experiences and another part through other people. We need to pray for the word we hear to be informed by a living understanding of how and when to act. We should stay humble, remembering that even though we are special to God, we are not the only spokesperson He has.

The Trap of Missed Timing

There is a *kairos* moment (perfect timing) for all things. If we talk about our word too soon, we might miss the Savior's timing and end up attempting to fulfill our word with second-rate results. We should remember what happened to Abraham and not birth an Ishmael because we just *could not wait* for an Isaac.

The Trap of Confusion

"God is not the author of confusion" (1 Corinthians 14:33 NKJV). Premature public chatting about all we have heard in private can result in confusion for ourselves as well as for others. To avoid the trap of confusion, we can set a guard over our heart and mouth and speak only those things that build up our hearers.

Oftentimes, God does tell us something ahead of time, before it comes into being. His word comes to prepare us and to change us to be the vessel qualified to do what has been spoken. We all seem to need to learn the hard way not to talk out of turn.

7. Know That God Will Confirm It

God will give us our own stuff—there is plenty to go around— but we can depend on the fact that God uses others to confirm His word. It is a part of His safety net of protection (2 Corinthians 13:1: "Every fact is to be confirmed by the testimony of two or three witnesses"). If it really is God speaking, He will speak the same or a similar thing more than once. I sigh with relief over that one. It helps to take the pressure off. In other words, you and I don't have to try to figure out what to do with a onetime word! If it really is from God, it will be confirmed. We can rest in that fact.

We can also trust that the Lord will speak through those in authority over us. If we are children living with our parents, we should pray for them. We can pray for our elders and pastors and those who are over them. A married woman should pray for her husband to have wisdom. Everyone should pray for those with whom they are going to take counsel. We need to bathe each situation in prayer. We can ask the Lord for trusted channels of authority in our lives, by which we can receive correction, encouragement, admonition and confirmation of what we believe God is saying. God will confirm His word to us through others. There is safety in many counselors (see Proverbs 15:22).

8. Beware of Counterfeits

Satan loves to counterfeit. He is not the Creator, so he has no originality; he is just a copycat! Think about what a counterfeit means. It implies that there is something authentic and real out there, something worth copying. There is counterfeit money because there is real money, and that real money has power.

The enemy counterfeits God's voice, and he counterfeits experiences, even rare, supernatural experiences. Why are the psychic hotlines so popular? Why does the New Age movement seem to have so much influence? People turn to psychics and New Age thinking because they so hungrily want to encounter the supernatural. People want guidance. People are born with a void that only the voice of God can fill. You want to hear His voice, too, or you would not be reading this book.

But beware of counterfeits from the dark side. Our vigilance is an important part of our equipment. While we remain vigilant, we can find reassurance in the fact that the very existence of counterfeit guidance proves that the Lord of hosts, who has the real power, also has the real thing—the real voice, the real dreams, myriad real angels and the true guidance system.

9. Practice Hearing God's Voice

Yes, practice hearing the voice of God, and it will become easier. It's like picking up the phone and recognizing the voice of a friend, whose voice you know because you have heard it so many times.

Years ago, I learned a lesson about this the hard way.

I am the youngest of three children. My oldest sister is six years older than I, and by the time I was in high school, she was long gone out of the home. Naturally, I did not know her very well.

Later, when I was at college, the phone rang one night, and I went out into the dorm hallway to answer it. There was an unfamiliar woman's voice on the other end of the phone. "Well, hello, James," she said. "How are you?"

"I'm fine," I said. "Uh, who is this?"

It was the voice of my older sister, Sandra, but I did not recognize it. I think it might have hurt her a bit that I did not recognize the voice of a member of my own family. I determined that I needed to get to know her voice before she called again!

In the same way, if I want to know the voice of the Holy Spirit, I have to spend some time with Him. When I said, "Uh, who is this?," I felt a tiny bit of what the holy Dove of God so often feels when He is overlooked and unrecognized. I want the voice of the Holy Spirit to become lovely to me. I never want to grieve Him. (By the way, I have a wonderful relationship with my older sister now, because I have come to know her dear voice and the heart with which she speaks.)

Get to know the voice of your Master by spending time "on the phone" with Him. Practice makes perfect.

10. Cultivate an Intimate Relationship

From God's perspective, the most important reason for hearing the voice of God is not so that we will know the right things to do but so that we will know Him, the source of the guidance.

True guidance involves getting closer to the Guide. We grow to know the Lord better as He speaks to us. As we listen to Him and obey His Word, our relationship with Him goes far beyond information, guidance, dreams, visions, angels and all the other wonderful supernatural stuff. The gifts of the Spirit are appetizers to whet our desire for more of God Himself.

The voice of God creates a deeper hunger within us so that we might come into closer communion with Him. The primary reason we need to hear His voice is really simple: to cultivate the intimate relationship with our Abba Father that He wants us to have.

Our Daddy God wants to commune with us even more than we want to commune with Him. Draw near, for He draws near to us. Now we have learned some of the strategic keys that are both practical and personal to help us hear God's voice more clearly today.

Heavenly Father, I want a vibrant relationship with You that is both personal and practical. I choose to submit every area of my life to You. Release the finger of God— the Holy Spirit—to point out any hindrances in my life and on my path. May the light of the Holy Spirit lead me out of any dimensions of darkness and bring me into Your marvelous light. Come, Holy Spirit, and magnify the voice of God in my life today. Amen, and amen!

THINK ABOUT IT

1. Which of the ten tools listed in this chapter do you need most to learn how to use? Which do you need to pick up right now?

2. Which of these tools do you find easiest to use? Why?

7

Walking in Community

If the foot says, "Because I am not a hand, I am not a part of the body," it is not for this reason any the less a part of the body. And if the ear says, "Because I am not an eye, I am not a part of the body," it is not for this reason any the less a part of the body. If the whole body were an eye, where would the hearing be? If the whole were hearing, where would the sense of smell be? But now God has placed the members, each one of them, in the body, just as He desired.

1 Corinthians 12:15–18

"A new commandment I give to you, that you love one another, even as I have loved you, that you also love one another. By this all men will know that you are My disciples, if you have love for one another."

John 13:34–35

Have you ever noticed the assortment of Christians at a large church gathering, a conference or a rally? As you scanned the crowd, have you dared to wonder what it will be like to spend time in heaven with all those folks? Awesome, right? Uh, now let's get real—there sure seem to be a lot of peculiar odds and ends out there. The funny thing is, these just happen to be our brothers and sisters in Christ. What will it be like to spend eternity with them? Or (gulp!) try to imagine spending eternity with the people you really know well.

There are occasions, I must admit, when I am judgmental of some of God's chosen ones—and, even worse, critical. Sometimes I look at the outside wrapper and swallow hard. I don't even know them and find myself already having a hard time with them. Yet I know that I will be spending eternity with them, and they with me, in heaven. By the grace of God, I will have His love for each and every one. I cannot claim to have it yet.

Each one of us is a jewel in the eyes of our Papa God. His Son, Jesus, loved us so much that He died for each one of us. Sometimes it is the most basic truths that we tend to forget.

Philip asked Jesus to show the disciples the Father (see John 14:8). Imagine the Son of God's disappointment, maybe even hurt, knowing they had not yet gotten the picture. In essence, He answers, "Hey, Philip, in case you didn't realize it in these past three years, the Father has been right here before you. If you have seen who I am, and if you have watched the works I have done, you have seen the Father" (see John 14:9). What had they witnessed? They had seen Him touch the lame and blind with compassion. They had seen Him hold the children in His arms. They had witnessed His tears. Whether He was healing, teaching, comforting or raising the dead, Jesus always exemplified the Father.

We are called to be witnesses, light and salt in this world. We are His children, and we are supposed to look, act and talk like

Him as His representatives on earth. But is the world able to see the Father's love in us? Moreover, can we see and hear our Papa God in and through our brothers and sisters?

A Diverse Body

One of the most common ways the Lord speaks is through the members of the Body of Christ—each and every one. I think God must have a lot of flat-out fun at times as He attempts to speak to us through our spouses, parents, children, neighbors and other odds and ends besides the ones we believe He is supposed to speak through. We accept the fact that our pastor or favorite Bible teacher at a conference or our church hears from God. But does God speak through Jerry, Susie or (fill in the name)? Each of us is so different. He made us that way. The Holy Spirit must find it a bit hard and yet fun and a little crazy sometimes to speak through all these different and unique vessels.

God loves diversity. He created all of life to display His passion for variety and His personal touch. We must be aware of this bent if we are to learn to hear Him through our brothers and our sisters. We each have our own quirks, comfort zones and preferences. Certain teachers talk our lingo. Some people just push all of our buttons the right way. We love to hear God's latest word through these people—and then there are the others. In all our lives, there will be the others, the ones who punch our buttons upside-down and ring our doorbells without mercy. Guess what? God Himself just might be at the door, and in our aggravation, we might miss Him.

Paul covers this tendency in 1 Corinthians 12:12–27. The Body of Christ has a diversity of parts, each one important to the whole. And yet the eye chatters to the foot, "Hey, I can't receive from you. You're not a part of my comfort zone." Why?

"You're one of those 'renewal people.'" The ear tells the knee, "Your church label has no room for what I've got to offer." The wrist declares to the hand, "Listen, honey, I'm the head of this house. I'm the spiritual leader here. I can move you any way I want. You just sit there and let me do the leading."

We all do it. We set our own strict little boundaries about how and through whom God can speak to us. We make a select list. Then, wham! Somebody messes with our list. We don't know what hit us, so we rebuke the devil. Later on, after we have become more humble, we learn it was God. Sometimes I wonder if He actually delights in messing with our lives, doctrines and perimeters. I know He has worked me over a few times.

An Unexpected Invasion

In 1992, the presence of the Lord invaded our house. His angels came. His presence was manifested in startling ways. At 11:59 p.m. on the Jewish Day of Atonement, a heavenly visitor came and stood in our bedroom and spoke to me as the clock turned to midnight. "I have come to speak with your wife," the visitor said. Not to me, mind you, but to my sweet wife, Michal Ann. The ensuing weeks of unusual divine encounters rocked our world, and the reverberations are still being felt today.

In our book *Encounters with a Supernatural God*, which later was revised to become *God Encounters*, Michal Ann told about this profound experience:

Beginning on the Day of Atonement, October 6, 1992, our family entered a nine-week period of supernatural visitations that forever changed our lives—especially mine. In retrospect, I suppose that period was like a compressed "pregnancy" in the spirit, measured in weeks instead of months. All I know is that by the time it was over, God had birthed a whole new identity in me that literally changed my relationship with Jim and revolutionized our approach to ministry.[1]

Those were interesting days, indeed. When I went out on the road ministering, I would call home to find out what God was saying! Here I had a certain reputation of being the one who could hear what the Lord was saying—but my wife? It was as though God had dried up my creek bed and I had to learn to hear through another channel.

As crazy as it no doubt sounds to many of you reading this today, the biggest lesson I learned in those days was so simple, but it radically changed my perspective on God, relationships, husbands and wives. "What lesson was that, James?" Glad you asked! I learned that God can to speak to and through whomever He wants whenever He wants. I mean, think about it. He chose to speak to Mary while keeping Joseph pretty much in the background. And He chose to speak to Michal Ann while I had been the one known for hearing God speak. My creek bed dried up, and hers became a torrential flood.

Do you know what this means? Maybe you—yes, you—are the next candidate God wants to invade with the glories of His brilliant presence!

An Unconventional Blend

When I came out of a traditional church and went into the Jesus Movement, it was very interesting to watch who accepted whom. Long-haired, hippie types were thrown in with the straitlaced types. All were authentic young converts on fire for God. It wasn't just that the conservative types rejected the radical element; it is also that many of those long-haired young people were not very receptive to those they considered staid and stuck in traditions. This happens throughout the Church in many ways. And yet all of us are Jesus People, carrying Jesus to others. To this day, I would say I am a Jesus People person!

Those who are versed in the history of the Church realize that God has often spoken through unusual vessels. Of course, back in the old days it was the norm. But if Jesus showed up in person today, what would He look like? If John the Baptist showed up at our Sunday-morning meeting or midweek Bible luncheon, how would we welcome the scruffy wilderness man with the booming voice? Imagine taking him to a local coffee shop to share a few honey-dipped locusts around one of those little tables. Soon everyone in the place would know how to repent for his or her sins.

Sooner or later, we learn a simple truth: Our Father God will use someone we would not. It might be a crabby neighbor, an actor on a TV show, an unsaved boss or our two-year-old child. He speaks through them all.

In *Encounters with a Supernatural God*, my wife wrote, "As believers in the one Body of Christ, we all need to learn how to listen to each other. We need to take a step back and let those rise to speak whom God has anointed for specific times and places."[2] Amen. Let it be so!

An Uncomfortable Word

Naaman was the captain of the army, a valiant warrior who served under the leadership of the king of Syria. He had a great reputation, except for one major problem—he was a leper. According to 2 Kings 5, Naaman's wife had a servant girl who had come from Israel; she had been captured during a war. The little girl knew of the ministry of the prophet Elisha. Innocently, the servant girl suggested to her mistress that her master, Naaman, go to Samaria to find the prophet Elisha.

Naaman made an appeal to the king of Syria and, surprisingly, was granted the request. The king of Syria sent his greatest warrior, Naaman, off to enemy territory carrying a letter asking that Naaman be healed. The king also sent Naaman along with an offering of ten talents of silver, six thousand shekels of gold and ten changes of clothes.

The king of Israel received Naaman, but of course he could not help him. Then Naaman went with his horses and his chariots and stood outside the doorway of the house of Elisha. But Elisha did not appear. Instead, he sent out a messenger with a word about what Naaman was to do. The instructions were, "Go and wash in the Jordan seven times, and your flesh will be restored to you and you will be clean" (verse 10). The nature of this response offended Naaman, and he "went away in a rage" (verse 12).

We can all identify with Naaman. Possibly, just possibly, there is a bit of his pride in each of us. We all have preconceived ideas about how God should answer our prayers. We expect God to speak one particular way. When He doesn't, off we run to throw a pity party. Remember the adage "God offends the mind to reveal the heart"?

Naaman's servants would not let him sulk. They sought him out and made an in-your-face appeal to him: "My father, had the prophet told you to do some great thing, would you not have done it? How much more then, when he says to you, 'Wash, and be clean'?" (verse 13).

Naaman must have been going through great inner turmoil. He was a proud man, but humility was being required of him in order to receive healing from the hand of the Lord. Such barriers also may stand in our way of receiving from our King.

To his credit, Naaman did humble himself. He obeyed. He went down and dipped himself seven times in the Jordan, according to the word of the man of God. His flesh was restored like the flesh of a little child, and he was healed. He heard and followed God's word, even when it was delivered by an ordinary servant and involved performing a seemingly meaningless task.

A Slew of Barriers

We each need to grow in the art of hearing God's voice through whatever ways and means God chooses to speak. But if we are honest, we realize that we have barriers that need to be identified and removed by His loving hand. The good news is that He is more than willing to help us. Following His lead, our barriers will eventually fall.

For example, I have had "women issues" in my past. But by the grace of God, and the help of my dear wife, many now consider me a champion for women in ministry. (I really had little choice. I could bless what the Father was doing or be left behind!)

The way I see it, some people seem to be HTRs while others tend to be ETRs. HTR stands for *hard to receive*, and ETR stands for *easy to receive*. HTRs—those who find it hard to receive God's word or His transforming help—should not be discouraged. My advice to HTRs is this: Spend lots of time simply worshiping God. Worship is a major key the Master has used to transform many hearts. Giant oak trees of stubbornness and fear fall before the transforming love of our Father. Theological backgrounds, traditions, cultures, ethnic origins, hurts and wounds of the past cannot withstand His light. God is bigger and brighter than all of our issues. When we stand before Him in worship, He has access to our spirits and our souls.

Common obstacles to hearing God's voice include:

- Lack of faith
- Lack of a strong commitment to Jesus as Lord
- The presence of sin
- Ignorance of the Scripture
- Lack of quality teaching
- Fear of man and rejection
- Fear of being deceived

- Guilty feelings
- Hurts from the past[3]

Many of these relate to other people. Like Adam and Eve, we hide behind fig leaves. But our fig leaves shield our hearts and souls just as effectively (or ineffectively) from God's approaching presence and thereby from true freedom.[4] They also obstruct our fellowship with others.

We can overcome any and all of the barriers that remain between God and us. There is healing for any ailment that has ever existed. The cure is as old as the universe itself. It is the love of God. Love heals.

How does healing happen? How can we get into the flow of our Father's love so that we can stop hiding from Him and really be able to hear His voice?

An Outpouring of Love

The Law reads, "You shall love the Lord your God with all your heart, and with all your soul, and with all your strength, and with all your mind; and your neighbor as yourself" (Luke 10:27). When Jesus came, He did not change that. He said, "Do this, and you will live" (verse 28).

If we want to see the barriers in our hearts and souls dissolve, we must ask the Holy Spirit to help us receive the gift of love that proceeds from our brothers and sisters. In a circular fashion, what goes around will come around. We will become a channel of God's love for them, too. We will hear God's voice for them, and they will hear it for us. Some of what we hear will be wordless—a kind of cleansing stream of healing love. Some of what we will hear will be very specific, and God's words will melt the barriers in our hearts, remove the log in our eye and lead us into all truth.

We are to love one another as the Father loved Jesus. The mutual love that exists in the Godhead is our example. The world is waiting to hear a clear sound from the Church. We have been in practice sessions tuning up long enough. Do you want the world to hear the voice of God? His voice is most fully audible when brothers and sisters in Christ love each other (see John 13:15).

Together, we make up the very Bride of Christ. Being a part of the Bride of Christ is more than just sitting next to someone in a church service or one of our great conference settings. Love has to be practical.

Recently I went through a very difficult battle. It was more than what my family and I could handle on our own. It was a battle with the big C-word—*cancer*. I had to cancel all my traveling engagements, so we had no income for our ministry team. But thank God for the Body of Christ. My family and I, usually the ones to be giving out love, were on the receiving end. It was a humbling experience—one in which I still hear the voice of God.

The big C of cancer was vanquished by God's multifaceted C: the community of Christ embraced the cross with compassion and care. Every evening for weeks, people brought us meals. Intercessors around the world lifted up prayers on our behalf. Believers enforced the victory of the cross of Christ over the powers of darkness. Encouraging words that came through emails, cards and people I had never met all merged together into an experience of the love of the Body of Christ. The outcome? The big C became a little *c*, and cancer bowed its knee at the name of Christ Jesus the Lord. Thank God for the Body of Christ and the finished work of the cross!

As we walk in the love of our brothers and sisters, we step out of the old chains that have prevented us from enjoying barrier-free intimacy with God. We will hear God's voice better with each passing year. We will become His mouthpieces to our unsaved loved ones and friends and to our neighborhoods, workplaces, cities and nations.

Guess what? We might even enjoy hearing God's voice through our brothers and sisters! If God lives in community with Himself (Father, Son and Holy Spirit), then should we not walk and live in community, as well?

Lord, I thank You for the Body of Christ and all those in spiritual authority. I thank You for my family members. Where I have a wrong independent spirit that causes me to run away from people and from You, point it out to me. This day, I choose to esteem the many different members of the Body of Christ. Give me a healthy community of believers to walk with and to learn from, in Jesus' name, Amen.

THINK ABOUT IT

1. Think of the names of your least-favorite brothers and sisters in Christ. Some may be family members. You may not be acquainted with others; perhaps you dislike them even though you have only read a book or heard a news report about them. It would help you hear God's voice if you could appreciate them with God's love, would it not? Ask God to give you His heart for the people you have named. He will answer your prayer.

2. Can you identify some of your fig leaves—the barriers behind which you hide? Again, can you bring these to your Father, trusting that He will help you with them?

8

Hearing with Discernment

"A stranger they simply will not follow, but will flee from him, because they do not know the voice of strangers."

John 10:5

Do not quench the Spirit; do not despise prophetic utterances. But examine everything carefully; hold fast to that which is good; abstain from every form of evil.

1 Thessalonians 5:19–22

But solid food is for the mature, who because of practice have their senses trained to discern good and evil.

Hebrews 5:14

A stranger they simply will not follow" (John 10:5). This chapter will help that statement become a reality for you. Let's learn to recognize the voice of God so well that all the other voices sound unfamiliar.

Let's not be like some people I know (and you probably know some, as well) who would benefit from some lessons in discernment. Instead of making the time to take driver's training classes, such people quickly get into the fastest car they can find and go off to the races. Some, sad to say, end up in a ditch or become casualties of driving without a license. Or they create problems with their zealous driving patterns and bump other cars off the path.

Let's avoid the ditches. Let's get our permits first, while being mentored by others sitting next to us, and then graduate to driving alone. Then let's repeat these safety lessons and help others with the very lessons we ourselves have learned. Where hearing God's voice is concerned, driver's education includes discernment lessons.

The Need for Discernment

The gift of discerning of spirits, which is listed in the New Testament as one of the gifts of the Spirit (see 1 Corinthians 12:10), is desperately needed in today's Church culture. This gift helps a believer distinguish what motivates spiritual activity. It helps a Christian see through the gray areas and differentiates light from darkness. C. Peter Wagner has defined the discerning of spirits as follows:

> The gift of discerning of spirits (or discernment) is the special ability that God gives to certain members of the body of Christ to know with assurance whether certain behavior purported to be God are in reality divine, human or satanic (Matthew 16:21–23; Acts 5:1–11; 16:16–18; 1 Corinthians 12:10; 1 John 4:1–6).[1]

In *The Beginner's Guide to Spiritual Gifts*, Sam Storms shares some examples of the gift of discerning of spirits in operation:

- Acts 16:16–18, where Paul discerned that the power of a certain slave girl was, in fact, a demonic spirit
- Acts 13:8–11, where Paul discerned that Elymas the magician was demonically energized in his attempt to oppose the presentation of the Gospel
- Acts 14:8–10, where again Paul discerned (by fixing his gaze on him) that a man had faith to be healed
- When a person is able to discern whether or not a problem in someone's life is demonic or merely the consequence of other emotional and psychological factors, or perhaps a complex combination of both
- When people with this gift are often able to detect or discern the presence of demonic spirits in a room or some such location
- Acts 8:20–24, where Peter was said to "see" (not physically, but through perceiving or sensing) that Simon Magus was filled with bitterness and iniquity
- It would seem that Jesus exercised something along the lines of this gift when he looked at Nathanael and described him as a man "in whom there is no deceit" (John 1:47). In John 2:25, it is said that Jesus "knew what was in man."[2]

Bottom line: This gift helps the believer see below the bottom line!

Think about it this way. When the outward appearance of a wolf is disguised, the human eye cannot immediately discern the wolf. However, a sheepdog will not be deceived, even by the sheep's clothing. He is not deceived because he does not judge by his eyesight but by his sense of smell. The wolf may look like a sheep, but he still smells like a wolf. In Scripture, discernment is like a sense of smell, acting independently of the natural eyesight.

Isaiah the prophet, foreseeing the ministry of Jesus as the Messiah, the anointed one, declares that "the spirit of the LORD . . . shall make him of quick understanding [literally, quick of scent] in the fear of the LORD: and he shall not judge after the sight of his eyes, neither reprove after the hearing of his ears" (Isaiah 11:2–3 KJV). Those to whom God commits the care of His sheep must likewise, through the Holy Spirit, be quick of scent.

Or think about it this way. What would you think if you had a spiritual experience that made your hair stand on end? Would you write it off as absolutely satanic or crazy because it did not fit into your theological grid? Consider some of the experiences of Daniel, Isaiah or Ezekiel that are recorded in the Old Testament. Daniel lay weary for days because of the impact of a supernatural vision (see Daniel 10:1–17). Isaiah had his lips seared by a burning coal (see Isaiah 6:1–7). Ezekiel was forced to lie on his side for 390 days straight (see Ezekiel 4:1–5). Then, in the New Testament, there are Zechariah, Paul and John, the beloved disciple. An angel strikes Zechariah dumb (see Luke 1:5–22), Paul is blinded (see Acts 9:1–9) and John sees visions of such magnitude that the entire book of Revelation is inadequate to record them.

We need the gift of discernment, don't we? Most of us in the Western world, if confronted with such events, would tend to chalk them up to psychological disturbances or the devil. Entire segments of the Body of Christ have written off hearing from the Lord because of their fear of being deceived and led astray. It is true that such experiences can come from the supernatural power of the enemy, from the human mind or from God Himself. Yet, as we have seen in this book, God wants us to recognize

His voice, and our Master is very capable of preserving us from harm and deception.

Jesus said:

> "For everyone who asks, receives; and he who seeks, finds; and to him who knocks, it shall be opened. Now suppose one of you fathers is asked by his son for a fish; he will not give him a snake instead of a fish, will he? . . . How much more will your heavenly Father give the Holy Spirit to those who ask Him?"
>
> Luke 11:10–11, 13

We can trust our Father. If we ask Him for the things of the Holy Spirit in the name of Christ, we will get the real things, not counterfeits. Two of His best gifts are wisdom and discernment. We need to stick close to Jesus and ask God to enable us to grow in these gifts!

Three Sources of Revelation

The Scriptures teach us that spiritual revelation or communication comes from one of three sources: the Holy Spirit, the human soul or the realm of evil spirits.

The Holy Spirit is the only true source of pure revelation. It was the Holy Spirit who moved the prophets of the Old Testament and the witnesses of the New Testament: "No [true] prophecy was ever made by an act of human will, but men moved by the Holy Spirit spoke from God" (2 Peter 1:21).

Thoughts, ideas and inspirations that don't originate with the Holy Spirit can be voiced by the human soul—the second source. These come out of the unsanctified portion of our emotions (see Jeremiah 23:16 and Ezekiel 13:1–6). As Ezekiel the prophet said, these are prophecies out of men's own hearts. He reported the words of God as he heard them: "Woe to the foolish prophets who are following their own spirit and have seen nothing" (Ezekiel 13:3).

The third source of revelation, evil spirits, can appear to be angels of light (good voices), but they always speak lies because they serve the chief liar and father of lies, Satan. Messages delivered through evil spirits are often especially dangerous to people ignorant of God's Word or inexperienced in discernment because Satan loves to mix just enough truth with his lies to trick gullible people.

Remember the slave girl with a spirit of divination described in Acts 16? She spoke the truth about the disciples, but she got her information from a satanic source. Eventually, the apostle Paul had heard enough. He was irritated (something just did not seem right!), and he commanded the spirit of divination to leave her. He discerned that her accurate revelations were coming from the wrong supernatural source. When the slave girl's owners became upset because their extra income had disappeared along with the evil spirit, Paul's discernment was confirmed. After all, God's servants do not sell their services as psychics.

Nine Tests of Revelation

The only way we can accurately and safely approach the interpretation of the motivation behind revelatory activity of any kind is to ask God for the spirit of wisdom and understanding. As we saw in chapter 3, "The Sound of Many Rushing Waters," God still speaks today through many different avenues, including visions, dreams, His inner voice, His audible voice, His creation and so forth. Yet our most important source of revelation is the canon of Scripture.

Since the Bible is our absolute standard against which we must test spiritual experiences, let's look at nine scriptural tests. I adapted these solid guidelines years ago into my own style from the ministry of the great British Bible teacher Derek Prince.

To be assured we are receiving accurate and valid revelation, we can apply the following list of nine scriptural tests:

1. *Does the revelation edify, exhort or console?* "But one who prophesies speaks to men for edification and exhortation and consolation" (1 Corinthians 14:3). The end purpose of all true revelation is to build up, admonish and encourage the people of God. It is summed up best in 1 Corinthians 14:26: "Let all things be done for edification."

2. *Is it in agreement with God's Word?* "All Scripture is given by inspiration of God" (2 Timothy 3:16 NKJV). Where the Holy Spirit has said yea and amen in Scripture, He also says yea and amen in revelation. He never contradicts Himself.

3. *Does it exalt Jesus Christ?* "He will glorify Me, for He will take of Mine and will disclose it to you" (John 16:14). All true revelation centers on the person of Jesus Christ and exalts Him (see Revelation 19:10).

4. *Does it have good fruit?* "Beware of the false prophets, who come to you in sheep's clothing, but inwardly are ravenous wolves. You will know them by their fruits" (Matthew 7:15–16). The true voice of God will produce fruit in character and conduct that agrees with the fruit of the Holy Spirit (see Galatians 5:22–23 and Ephesians 5:9).

5. *If it predicts a future event, does it come to pass?* "When a prophet speaks in the name of the LORD, if the thing does not come about or come true, that is the thing which the LORD has not spoken. The prophet has spoken it presumptuously; you shall not be afraid of him" (Deuteronomy 18:22). Two of the major areas where people make

mistakes are the setting of dates and the predicting of events. This should be left to the more mature while giving grace for the learning curves in each of our lives.

6. *Does the revelation turn people toward God or away from Him?* (See Deuteronomy 13:1–5.) If a person's words seem to be accurate but end up turning people away from following Jesus Christ as the Son of God, then it is a mistake to adhere to his or her ministry.

7. *Does it produce liberty or bondage?* "For you have not received a spirit of slavery leading to fear again, but you have received a spirit of adoption as sons by which we cry out, 'Abba! Father!'" (Romans 8:15). True revelation given by the Holy Spirit produces liberty, not bondage (see 1 Corinthians 14:33 and 2 Timothy 1:7).

8. *Does it produce life or death?* "For the letter kills, but the Spirit gives life" (2 Corinthians 3:6). The authentic voice of God always produces growth and life-giving energy, not hopelessness, stagnation or defeat.

9. *Does the Holy Spirit bear witness that it is true?* "As for you, the anointing which you received from Him abides in you, and you have no need for anyone to teach you; but as His anointing teaches you about all things, and is true and is not a lie, and just as it has taught you, you abide in Him" (1 John 2:27). The Holy Spirit is called "the Spirit of truth" (John 16:13). His indwelling presence in our hearts and minds provides us with a kind of supernatural common sense about the accuracy of words that seem to be from God. This ninth test is the most subjective and therefore must be used in conjunction with the previous eight standards.

These nine scriptural tests might seem elementary to you. I am glad if they do. They are supposed to be foundational.

Absorb these biblical guidelines into your life and apply them to other areas of life and ministry. Then teach others these basic principles of receiving and discerning accurate and valid revelation, and we will all be winners.

The Need for Surrendered Senses

Have you ever seen or felt or discerned a supernatural presence by the Holy Spirit—whether it be angelic or a demonic one? When we "see" or "sense" or "feel" a spiritual entity nearby, we have *discerned* its presence. Hebrews 5:14 says, "But solid food is for the mature, who because of practice have their senses trained to discern good and evil." This is about the training of our senses, which help us discern. They are a key component of the process.

Surrendering our senses to the Holy Spirit involves the very act of presenting the members of our physical body to God (see Romans 6:13, 19). We sanctify each of our five natural senses to the Holy Spirit. We surrender everything we have to Him to be used for His divine purposes. To whom we present our members, to them they become a slave. So, let's present our entire being unto God as an act of worship (see Romans 12:1–2).

This act of presentation is so very vital if we are going to be able to distinguish the spiritual origins of supernatural realities. It is a key to accurately moving in a higher realm of the anointing of the Holy Spirit. Surrendering and presenting our natural five senses to the Dove of God is a very specific and necessary part of the process.

You can be empowered by God to discern both good and bad spiritual beings, manifestations and operations. The very presence of the Lord Himself will then rest upon our natural senses and enable us to feel, hear, taste, smell and see in another realm. We move from the natural into the supernatural!

In general, discernment always involves the evaluation of some kind of evidence. We can only accomplish this by using our five bodily senses: sight, hearing, smell, taste or touch. We notice something; then we start sifting through the incoming data. We discriminate between the pieces of evidence, and we detect patterns. Then we decide what to do, based in large part on what our discernment tells us.

Again, the discerning (or distinguishing) of spirits is one of the gifts of the Holy Spirit (1 Corinthians 12:10). This gift is a little different from the gift of the word of knowledge, in which facts are simply dropped into our minds or hearts. With discernment, you have to consider what is happening around you. Did what just happened make you afraid or full of faith? Did the room just get brighter or darker? Did you hear a noise? Did you perhaps smell or taste something? Is what happened from a good source or a bad one?

To discern spiritual realities, we need spiritual perception. To flow in the prophetic, to see people get healed, to see people be set free from demonic bondages, we need God's supernatural anointing. We need to detect the very source working behind the scenes. Is this thing just your imagination, or is it coming from someone else's human spirit? Is the source of the manifestation demonic? Is it, in fact, an angel? Is it the Holy Spirit?

God does not just take the gift of discerning of spirits and plug it into you, fully developed. Normally, it takes a lot of practice to get good at this, and some of your "discernment lessons" will involve making mistakes. This is why it so clearly states in the strategic Hebrews 5:14 verse that mature believers "because of practice have their senses trained to discern good and evil." Practice makes us stronger at this—so let's take practice lessons today! If it was good enough for the writer of the book of Hebrews, then it is good enough for you and me.

Practice is a normal aspect of any learning process, and all the more when it comes to discernment and flowing in the supernatural life. This is part of your maturation as a disciple of Jesus, which always stems from Bible study, experience and discipline. Don't forget—you can always ask God to give you more ability to discern spirits and to grow into greater maturity. He wants this for us more than we want it ourselves!

Join with me in the surrendering of senses to the Holy Spirit. Together, let's become more mature in our ability to hear with discernment for Jesus Christ's sake. Let's press on to the upward call in God.

May God give us the ability to walk in the grace of discerning His voice from all the other voices of strangers. May we each experience the fullness of the spirit of wisdom and revelation in the knowledge of our Lord Jesus Christ (see Ephesians 1:17–19). Let's pause now to close out this strategic chapter with a prayer for His providential help.

Father God, Your Word tells me to not despise prophesying, to test all things and to hold fast to what is good. Teach me to discern Your voice. I lift up Your Word as my standard. Help me to be a wise steward of Your grace, dear Lord. Teach me to discern good from evil. Grant me an appropriate fear of You and the wisdom to judge revelation properly. In Jesus' mighty name, Amen.

THINK ABOUT IT

1. Read Acts 10, the story of Peter and Cornelius. Apply the nine scriptural tests to Peter's vision. Does his experience pass the tests?

2. Wisdom (which helps us know what to do next) goes hand in hand with discernment (which helps us know the source of what we observe). Are you stronger in one of these qualities than in the other? Are you lacking in one or both of them? Do you have trusted friends who can help you compensate for your relative weakness by giving wise counsel or by confirming your own discernment?

9

He Will Guide You!

Although the Lord has given you the bread of privation and water of oppression, He, your Teacher will no longer hide Himself, but your eyes will behold your Teacher. Your ears will hear a word behind you, "This is the way, walk in it," whenever you turn to the right or to the left.

Isaiah 30:20–21

Your word is a lamp to my feet and a light to my path.

Psalm 119:105

"But when He, the Spirit of truth, comes, He will guide you into all the truth; for He will not speak on His own initiative, but whatever He hears, He will speak; and He will disclose to you what is to come."

John 16:13

Do you remember playing the Hot or Cold game as a child? You would be blindfolded, and some object in the room would be selected by the others for you to try to find as you blindly groped around the room. Your playmates would shout, "You're getting warmer! Naw, you're *cold*. Warm . . . warmer . . . hot!" Of course, *hot* meant you were getting closer to the desired object, and *cold* meant you were going in the wrong direction.

The Geiger counter works a little bit like that game. It is an interesting instrument, named for Hans Geiger, the German physicist who invented it in 1928. The Geiger counter can detect the presence and intensity of radiation (the spontaneous emission of energy from radioactive elements, most notably uranium) by using a gas-filled tube that briefly conducts electricity when radiation makes the gas conductive. The Geiger counter amplifies this signal into a series of clicks. The closer it gets to the radioactive substance and the greater the intensity of the substance's radiation, the louder and faster the clicking noise becomes.

I have often thought this is a lot like our approach to hearing God's voice. Our spirit is like the Geiger counter that tells us whether we are closer or further away. It helps us put all the pieces together. We learn to pay attention to an inner witness. We check in with the Holy Spirit, we listen to our "knower," and our spirit either bears witness or it doesn't. When we are filled with the Holy Spirit, we have a divine guidance system that comes as part of the package, and we need that guidance system to get to the right result.

Are you getting warmer—closer to what God wants to say? Or are you getting colder—further away from it? Do you pay attention to the signals? How well do you navigate the maze of voices vying for your attention? The following principles will guide you along your way.

Determining God's will is more an art form than a science. It is not as much about equations as it is about principles. Yet there are basic precepts of which we each need to be aware. They are some of the signals that will help us zero in on God's true word.

In this chapter, we are going to cover ten principles of divine guidance. Some of the principles will be a bit of review, and some will be fresh and new. Let these ten principles of divine guidance help you hear God's voice today, determine His guidance and, most of all, grow closer to God Himself.

Principle 1: The Will of God Is Made Known in the Word of God

Some people start trying to listen to the subjective without being grounded first in the objective. They don't have a gauge to judge what they are sensing, hearing, feeling, thinking or what I call knowing. Here is a very basic example: Let's say that one day we read in Exodus 20:14, "You shall not commit adultery." That registers in our spirit and stays there. Not long afterward, we are walking in the mall and we see a very attractive person of the opposite sex. Some inner voice suggests something like, *Look over there at that good-looking person. Wow!* But because the Scripture is hidden in our heart, it is easy to turn away from that thought.

We don't even have to spend much time evaluating whether that tempting voice is God's; we know it is not. The Word (the objective *logos*) is hidden in our heart, and it informs us that this stray thought should be ignored—that it is, in fact, the beginning of a temptation. In all guidance, God's Word is the final judge. Let God's Word have the final say.

Principle 2: The Will of God Is Confirmed through Circumstances

During my senior year of college, I was quite zealous for the Lord. I read a tract on expelling demons and went and did it that day. It worked! Although earlier I had given myself much more to my studies, I then became a full-blown Jesus nut, and I cared little about the pursuit of academic credentials. I was ready to quit college at the end of my first trimester of my senior year, although I needed only twenty more hours to complete my degree.

My grades were still good, but they were not the high honors that they had once been. I thought I was ready for full-time ministry. On with it! Forget this mundane stuff. So I prayed something like this:

> O God, I just want to forget this stuff and get on with my real calling! But if You want me to finish out this year, I ask You to do something. Show me Your will!

Then a surprising thing happened. Even though I was considering quitting school that fall, with only nine months to go until graduation, somehow I received a scholarship for which I had not even applied. It was a religious leadership scholarship to help me financially so that I could complete the rest of my year at a secular university. So I decided, *That's a pretty good circumstantial sign. God has answered. I'd better go ahead and complete what I have started!*

I am glad I completed that degree in social work. I might not have met my wife if I hadn't. Now, that would have been a disappointment, for sure!

Circumstances alone do not constitute divine guidance, but they can often confirm God's will. Do not use this principle as your sole source of guidance, but know that it is one of the ways of the Holy Spirit yesterday, today and tomorrow.

Principle 3: The Holy Spirit Speaks from Where He Dwells

Where does God dwell? Not only does He dwell in heaven, but He also dwells within us if we are children of God and we have been filled with the Holy Spirit. According to 1 Corinthians 6:19, "Your body is a temple of the Holy Spirit who is in you." Colossians 1:27 confirms, "Christ *in you, the hope of glory.*" He speaks to us from where He dwells, which is in us.

Have you listened to your heart lately? What is beating in your heart? John 16:13 states, "But when He, the Spirit of truth, comes, He will guide you into all the truth; for He will not speak on His own initiative, but whatever He hears, He will speak; and He will disclose to you what is to come."

The Holy Spirit is heaven's representative in all true guidance. Through the Holy Spirit, Jesus not only resides at the Father's right hand; if you are a born-again believer, Jesus lives inside of your heart. Now, that is good news. But the principle I have given you here is that the Holy Spirit speaks from where He dwells. So, we must learn to push the pause button and quiet the external noises around us in order to listen. According to Psalm 46:10, "Be still, and know that I am God" (NKJV). It is simple but true: Communication is a two-way street. Hush up long enough to listen to the voice of the Holy Spirit speaking within your very own heart!

Principle 4: Divine Guidance Comes from Meeting God's Conditions

What are the divine conditions that must be met for guidance to be unlocked? Has He heard our cry? If we meet His conditions, He will surely guide us. Second Chronicles 7:14 paints this principle for us rather clearly: "If my people, who are called by my name, will humble themselves and pray and seek my face and turn from their wicked ways, then I will hear from heaven, and I will forgive their sin and will heal their land" (NIV). Notice the *if* that is clearly stated before the promise is given.

So, what are God's conditions? Read Isaiah 58, where we find

119

some of God's requirements described. The chapter speaks about honoring God and caring for the downtrodden, observing the Sabbath and not pointing the finger in accusation of others. Above all, we see that having a humble heart is of the utmost importance.

If our attitude toward God and our fellow human beings is not arrogant, then God's corresponding promise is, "And the LORD will continually guide you" (Isaiah 58:11). When the conditions are met, then the promise comes tumbling forth.

Principle 5: Peace of God Accompanies True Guidance

Peace does not mean there is no storm. Peace does not mean there is no warfare, either. God's peace creates a center of quiet in the midst of turbulence. True guidance from God does not push us; it brings peace and satisfaction. James remarks, "The wisdom from above is first pure, then peaceable, gentle, reasonable, full of mercy and good fruits, unwavering, without hypocrisy" (James 3:17).

Notice that James states that the wisdom of God is unwavering. That is an interesting interjection. It means God does not say one thing one day and something totally different the next. The Holy Spirit's guidance is constant and unwavering. It can be tested by time and tested by content. God's guidance is not nervous or tentative. God is not the author of confusion but of steadfastness and peace.

According to Romans 14:17, "The kingdom of God is not eating and drinking, but righteousness and peace and joy in the Holy Spirit." If God's voice is an instrument of His Kingdom, then His voice speaks peace, not chaos.

Principle 6: Much Guidance from God Comes Unnoticed

Much of our guidance comes undetected. We are often unaware that we are being guided. This is because we have asked God to continually guide us. He wants us to do His will even more than we want to do it. Isn't that a great thought to ponder? He will guide us continually.

This principle is also true because of the sovereignty of God. He is quietly releasing His thoughts into our sanctified minds so that we can make wise decisions. I love the great hymns of the church. Consider this poetic line: "His eye is on the sparrow, and I know He watches me." All I can say is yes and amen!

When it comes to this realm of divine guidance, humility is another subtle key that unlocks God's provision: "He leads the humble in justice, and He teaches the humble His way" (Psalm 25:9). In response to this, let's offer God this prayer:

Thank You, Lord, for Your gentle nudges, whispers in the night and occasional pushes and shoves. Thank You for guiding us even when we cannot tell that it is You.

Principle 7: Divine Guidance Does Not Mean We Know All the Details

You might read the title of this principle and think, *That is not what I want to hear!* We prefer to be able to know everything, don't we?

Each of us is like a child who wants to see a great parade that is coming down the street, only there is a tall fence separating the child from the parade. The child is not tall enough to see over the fence. He or she can hear the sound of it coming. It sounds exciting, and the child wants to see it. The child gets excited, then frustrated, but suddenly he or she finds a little knothole in the fence. Now as the child is looking through the knothole, the parade is passing by, and he or she spots a funny clown. The child is so excited, thinking, *Oh, I just love this parade; this is just wonderful.*

Only the next time the child takes a peek, he or she does not see anything. Why? Because there is a gap between parade events. Now the child says, "I think it's all over." But it isn't over at all; it is just a pause.

The child can still hear the music, so he or she takes another look. This time there is a new problem. Somebody is standing in the way. The child may stomp his or her feet and throw a fit, or the child may decide to poke a stick through the hole and say, "Hey, you. Move!" We could say the child has issues of character development and that he or she is learning patience.

Now the child turns, and something else catches his or her attention—a ladder going up the side of the house. The child scrambles up the ladder to the top of the roof. From this rooftop view, the child can see the beginning, the middle, all the way to the end of the parade.

It is the same with God's guidance. We want the rooftop view. And the Lord wants us, in a sense, to have the rooftop view we so much desire. But most of the time, we only get to look through the knotholes in the fence. There may be a special time when we see A, B, C and even a portion of X, Y and Z. Those awesome experiences can ruin us for life (in a good way).

But most of the time, we will only see what is in front of us. That is just the way it is. It keeps us reliant on God and humble. Just the same, we can enjoy the parade. Go with what the lamp of God's Word is already revealing, and His light will give you more every step of the way (see Psalm 119:105).

Principle 8: The Process of Guidance Is Not Always Pleasant

In Isaiah 55:8–9, God declares:

> "My thoughts are not your thoughts, nor are your ways My ways," declares the LORD. "For as the heavens are higher than the

earth, so are My ways higher than your ways and My thoughts than your thoughts."

The New Testament teaches us that we can have the "mind of Christ" (1 Corinthians 2:16). But there is a noticeable gap between our thoughts, opinions, reasoning and traditions, and His. We are unaccustomed to His ways. We think He should do things in a certain order, and He seems to like to mess that up. God's guidance might not seem to be very pleasant, because we experience heartbreak and disappointment.

Sometimes the voice of the Lord and His guidance system is like that proverbial sand in the oyster. It is an irritant to begin with. But give it some time and room to do its work, and a pearl of great price will emerge.

If we choose His way over our way, it might seem painful for the moment, but the end result will be good.

Principle 9: Hearing God Speak Should Prompt Us to Action

God's word is compelling. If we act on it, we will hear more. In Daniel 11:32 we read, "But the people who know their God will display strength and take action." God's word works in us. I love the acronym ACT, which stands for Action Changes Things. It is true. As Michal Ann and our oldest son, Justin, used to say, "Just do something!"

Many times people are looking for the next word from God. Well, I have a majorly important word of wisdom straight from the throne of God for you. The word for today is: Have you done the last thing God spoke? What was the last thing God told you to do? Have you completed it?

Don't be overcome by a sense of failure. Ask God for another chance. I have been learning our God is the God of the *fiftieth* chance, not only the second chance. His mercies are new every morning. Please learn from the past, but forget what lies behind and press forward into the upward call of Christ Jesus. I have even had to take my losses and present them to God and trust that He will cause all things to work together for good (see Romans 8:28).

Principle 10: Guidance Is a Skill to Be Learned over a Lifetime

If we have heard God speak once, we cannot assume we have learned how to hear Him once and for all. We are on a lifetime walk with Him. And remember the lessons from the earlier chapter about the sound of many rushing waters. There are always more classes to take in the School of the Spirit that teach us to hear God's voice today.

Here's another nugget that might help. I learned early on that I could hear the Holy Spirit's voice for other people. It is a great privilege and responsibility to be gifted in such a manner. But when it comes to getting guidance for myself, I don't seem to hear Him in the same manner. I hear Him the same way others hear Him for themselves: through my relationship with Him. Yes, it always boils down to a two-way walkie-talkie.

I should cultivate the gifts of the Holy Spirit so that God can use me to release blessings to others. But to really grow in the very subjective art of hearing God for myself, I need to be like John the beloved and lean my head upon the chest of my Messiah and Master, listening for the very heartbeat of God. You and I need to cultivate a friendship with Jesus. Then we will be able to hear God in all His multifaceted modes of expression. We will find that true guidance is not just a onetime thing. Hearing the voice of God depends on having a lifetime relationship, and that can never be taken away. It is walking with the Guide Himself.

As we review God's principles and grow in loving Him, our internal Geiger counter will become more and more reliable. It will guide us to the source of power, even when the light seems dim and it is hard to find the way. Yes, we are each given a Geiger counter of guidance. We just need to learn to turn it on and use it.

We each need help in navigating through the maze of life. So, once again, we turn to God and echo these words back into His heart:

Lord, I want to be led by Your Spirit and hear Your voice speaking more clearly. Tune me in to Your voice. Grant me the supernatural ability to discern Your voice from the voice of the stranger. Guide me. Be my navigation system to help me through the maze of life so that I get to where You want me to be and do what You want me to do. Lead me and guide me into Your will and Your ways, in Jesus' great name, Amen.

THINK ABOUT IT

1. Choose one of the ten principles of divine guidance and tell somebody how it has worked for you. If you don't have someone to tell, write down your thoughts about how you relied on the principle.

2. With informed hindsight, reflect on a circumstance in your life that illustrates principle six, which says that much guidance from God comes unnoticed. What guidance has come that you acknowledge now but did not recognize in the moment?

10

Listening, Waiting and Watching

The Lord GOD has given Me the tongue of disciples, that I may know how to sustain the weary one with a word. He awakens Me morning by morning, He awakens My ear to listen as a disciple. The Lord GOD has opened My ear; and I was not disobedient nor did I turn back.

Isaiah 50:4–5

Those who wait for the LORD will gain new strength; they will mount up with wings like eagles, they will run and not get tired, they will walk and not become weary.

Isaiah 40:31

I will stand on my guard post and station myself on the rampart; and I will keep watch to see what

He will speak to me, and how I may reply when I
am reproved. Then the LORD answered me and said,
"Record the vision and inscribe it on tablets, that
the one who reads it may run. For the vision is yet
for the appointed time; it hastens toward the goal
and it will not fail. Though it tarries, wait for it; for
it will certainly come, it will not delay."

Habakkuk 2:1–3

Hearing God's voice today is a very natural act but requires the activity of a supernatural God. There is no autopilot setting that guarantees that you will hear. One truth is that if you do nothing, you will receive nothing. But the seemingly opposite truth is also true: When you least qualify and least expect it, God shows up! While I emphasize that all good things come by grace, I also teach that we must add works to our faith to be effective (see James 2:26). These are two sides of the same coin.

Some years ago, I was teaching on the related subject of contemplative prayer and introducing one of my books, titled *The Lost Art of Practicing His Presence.* I was explaining that the book was a contemporary read on the spiritual disciplines. Problem is, the Holy Spirit interrupted me while I was publicly speaking and said to me, *Discipline? You do not have enough discipline to have a spiritual discipline.*

Now, what was I supposed to do? The Holy Spirit had nailed me, and I knew it. But I had just written and released this deeper book on what I believed were the spiritual disciplines.

Thank God the Holy Spirit did not leave me shocked and stunned right there in front of everyone. Rather, He shared an amazing principle with me as He continued to instruct me with His voice, saying, *They're not spiritual disciplines, anyway; they're spiritual privileges.* Case closed! Was I ever relieved, and did I ever learn an important dynamic principle that I hold close to my heart to this day.

Yes, hearing God's voice today includes some basic dos and don'ts, but it is not about a list of deeds to be done out of religious obligation. Hearing God's life-changing voice is an amazing privilege based in a loving relationship with our heavenly Father. It is a delight and an honor, not a religious act built on some performance-based acceptance.

Three Key Invitations

Ready to level up to some master's-level classes in the School of the Spirit? The following passage has guided my life with Papa God for many years and can provide you with further tools, as well, when it comes to this relational art form of communing with God and hearing His voice today:

> "Now therefore, O sons, listen to me, for blessed are they who keep my ways. Heed instruction and be wise, and do not neglect it. Blessed is the man who *listens* to me, *watching* daily at my gates, *waiting* at my doorposts. For he who finds me finds life and obtains favor from the LORD."
>
> Proverbs 8:32–35, emphasis added

Three key words are used in this passage in the passive, continuous tense: 1) *listens*, 2) *watching* and 3) *waiting*. This is not a onetime deal we are talking about. These three verbs invite us into an ongoing, intimate relationship that lasts a lifetime.

We will develop these three principles more as we go along in this chapter. But first, let me give you a promise also revealed here in this passage. The promise is found in verse 35: "For he who finds me finds life." Isn't that exciting? God's voice brings *life* to us!

But that is not all. There is still more. Verse 35 goes on to say, ". . . and obtains favor from the LORD." Mercy! Life and favor—what promises! This is a far cry from obligatory religious duty. God desires us to experience real life and favor. That stuns me to this day. It is just like the Holy Spirit said to me that day: *They're not spiritual disciplines, anyway; they're spiritual privileges.*

Now, in my writings, I attempt to weave three diverse strands of truth together to create my treasured tapestry. One thread I weave into my loom is detailed scriptural research; a second thread is the precedent set by Jewish and Church history; a third strand is modern-day, contemporary experiences found in the lives of others or in my own God encounters. With this in mind, let's take a glance at how these principles are found in a couple of these colorful threads.

In the Life of Joshua

Moses chose young Joshua for a long apprenticeship, through which he became a steward of the promises given to one generation and fulfilled in the next generation. With this backdrop, let's consider an example of the interconnected lives of Moses and Joshua as it pertains to the subject of listening, waiting and watching. For this, let's turn to Exodus 33:7–11:

> Now Moses used to take the tent and pitch it outside the camp, a good distance from the camp, and he called it the tent of meeting. And everyone who sought the LORD would go out to the tent of meeting which was outside the camp. And it came about, whenever Moses went out to the tent, that all the people would arise and stand, each at the entrance of his tent, and gaze after Moses until he entered the tent. Whenever Moses entered the tent, the pillar of cloud would descend and stand at the entrance of the tent; and the LORD would speak with Moses. When all the people saw the pillar of cloud standing at

the entrance of the tent, all the people would arise and worship, each at the entrance of his tent. Thus the LORD used to speak to Moses face to face, just as a man speaks to his friend. When Moses returned to the camp, his servant Joshua, the son of Nun, a young man, would not depart from the tent.

Moses not only had a powerful public ministry, but he maintained his personal private ministry. He would enter into the tent of meeting to minister to and spend time with the Lord God Himself. God would speak to Moses there. (What a great example demonstrating a strategic key to hearing God's voice today. Moses took time apart to be with God, and God spoke directly to him. Imagine what could happen if we did the same!) The bulk of the followers would acknowledge Moses' activity, but only at a distance. When Moses was no longer visible, they would return to their tents and carry out their business as usual—well, at least until the pillar of fire with signs and wonders appeared, after which they worshiped at their own tents, of course.

Then there was the exception of the day: young Joshua, who would wait at the entrance of the tent of meeting. He did not go anywhere. I have no idea how long he waited. But it paid off, as young Joshua would be the first to see the penetrating reflection of God's glory on Moses' face.

Joshua was thus schooled in the lost art of listening, waiting and watching daily at the gates. He observed firsthand the lessons related to hearing God's voice and encountering the fiery presence of God. This set Joshua aside from all the others and postured him to be an inheritor of the promises of the preceding generation.

Positioning ourselves at the feet of Jesus—this listening, waiting and watching—will do this for us, as well. We will see the face of Jesus, and the radiance of God's light shall shine upon us, as it did between Moses and Joshua.

In the Life of David

My late wife, Michal Ann, loved the psalms and read them every day of her life. The passage that guided her life the most was contained in Psalm 84. In fact, this psalm is inscribed on her tombstone in the quiet and peaceful Dover Cemetery in rural Missouri.

Let me direct us to one selected verse from Psalm 84: "For a day in Your courts is better than a thousand outside. I would rather stand at the threshold of the house of my God than dwell in the tents of wickedness" (verse 10). I can only imagine the glory of such an experience.

Now, when it comes to the life of David, this psalm practically shouts his name. He is not the author of this particular psalm, but in looking at his life, it becomes obvious he knew perhaps better than anyone the art of waiting at the threshold of the door of the house of God. We could even assume his goal in life was to be a doorkeeper for the Lord. Few people could say they were a psalmist, a shepherd of the flocks, a warrior, a prophet and a king, but David could. I wonder if his harp-and-bowl ministry before the Lord is what caught the Father's eye. Could that be why the Scriptures say David had God's own heart (see Acts 13:22)?

I have made it my goal to be a doorkeeper for the Lord, as well. While I am known for my public ministry, the posture and function I value the most is my place before Him. Oh, how I love to hear His voice. What I love even more is simply being with Him. Hearing Jesus' voice is merely a by-product of hanging out with Him! I encourage you to carve out some "hang time," as well.

In My Life with My Bride

"Where do I begin to tell to the story of how great a love can be?" These haunting, poetic words begin the romantic theme song from the 1970 award-winning movie *Love Story*, starring Ali MacGraw and Ryan O'Neal. I relate to that movie, not just because I was a '70s child, but because of its classic portrayal of a love that never fades and never fails. I shared such a love with my bride, Michal Ann, who passed away in 2008.

One of my fondest memories of my time with Michal Ann happened in the last three months of her life on this side of heaven. I remember the early morning when, in her weakened state, we sat together in our rocking chairs on the front porch of our amazing southern house, drinking organic green tea. We said nothing the entire time; we just listened. "Just listened? To what?" some inquire. Oh, to the sounds of silence. We listened to the morning dew glistening on the grass. We listened to the sun rising. We watched the rays of light melt away the fog on our pond at a distance down the hill.

Suddenly, as we sat there in silence, an entire charm of hummingbirds came flitting around the feeder near us. We quietly counted 29 hummingbirds hovering there, all at one time! Unprecedented, indeed. The sound of their fluttering wings astounded us as we sat in awe and wonder at God's creation. What is more, hummingbirds were Michal Ann's favorite species, and 29 was her special number in her personal relationship with her Lord. That moment is a miracle etched in my memory, and it happened as we simply listened, waited and watched.

Keep on Listening

So, yes, keep on listening. When you take time to shut the door and commune with God, you will hear wonderful words of life—wonderful words meant for you and you alone.

I encourage you to pray the verses of Isaiah 50:4–5 over your own life:

The Lord GOD has given me the tongue of disciples, that I may know how to sustain the weary one with a word. He awakens Me morning by morning, He awakens my ear to listen as a disciple. The Lord GOD has opened My ear; and I was not disobedient, nor did I turn back.

Ask that you be given a listening ear. Declare that He has given you the tongue of a disciple as a result of having an awakened ear. But remember, too, that this is about an intimate relationship, not just great technique. We do not hear in the exact same manner as everybody else, and the way God speaks to us in one season might be different in the next. But keep on listening!

When it comes to listening, three of Jesus' disciples had front seats in a master's-level course on listening at the Mount of Transfiguration. Mark 9:1–8 gives us the entire story line, but let's look closely at just one small portion: "Then a cloud formed, overshadowing them, and a voice came out of the cloud, 'This is My beloved Son, listen to Him!' All at once they looked around and saw no one with them anymore, except Jesus only" (Mark 9:7–8). These two verses depict the jealousy of the Father for His Son. They demonstrate His great longing to speak to us. Furthermore, when it comes down to it, the disciples saw no one else, only Jesus.

In order to hear God, we must learn to deal with distraction. The key is to be so focused on Him that everything else fades in the background. The disciples could have gotten caught up in lengthy discussions about the past or present moves of God (Moses—the Law; and Elijah—the prophets). But the Father directed their eyes to see Jesus only. We, too, need a revelation of His loveliness. This is a higher path than just resisting evil. When we see and know God's love, then we will stop and listen. Keep on listening.

Keep on Watching

While there are many appropriate texts to reference the vast subject of watching, let's take a glance at Habakkuk 2:1–3:

> I will stand on my guard post and station myself on the rampart; and I will keep watch to see what He will speak to me, and how I may reply when I am reproved. Then the LORD answered me and said, "Record the vision and inscribe it on tablets, that the one who reads it may run. For the vision is yet for the appointed time; it hastens toward the goal and it will not fail. Though it tarries, wait for it; for it will certainly come, it will not delay."

We notice from this passage that watching is an active event. We stand at our guard post and watch for what the Lord will say. When He finally speaks, we receive our marching orders. But will we be patient until He speaks? Will we keep watch? Will we not give up our station?

The proper inner attitude is the key that unlocks our ability to hear and see in the Spirit. Watching could be considered both a gift and an art that must be learned. This is a combination, then, of gifting and character development.

In Matthew 26:40, Jesus asked His disciples the piercing question, "Could you not watch with Me one hour?" (NKJV). Notice He does not just say, "Pray!" Instead, He tells them to watch. This is an important posture to learn in our praying—and, thus, hearing.

One of the greatest prophetic words ever given to me was not released publicly or even verbally. It was shipped to my home right after I had engaged in a speaking ministry in Mobile, Alabama. It came in the form of a framed picture and was sent to me by an elderly prophetic statesman. The picture, though given to me many years ago, still hangs in my house to this day. It is a portrayal of a man who has fallen asleep on his watch on the wall. Hordes of enemies are approaching to take the city as the watcher was asleep. The words of Ezekiel 33:6 are written out on the picture:

> "But if the watchman sees the sword coming and does not blow the trumpet and the people are not warned, and a sword comes and takes a person from them, he is taken away in his iniquity; but his blood I will require from the watchman's hand."

This remains a constant reminder to me to be alert on my watch for and with Him. Keep on watching!

Keep on Waiting

Let's take one more class in our master's-level course studies on hearing God's voice today. After Listening 101, we patiently partook of Watching 202. Now it's time for Waiting 303. Our primary text that we will consider comes from Isaiah 30:18–21:

> Therefore the LORD longs to be gracious to you, and therefore He waits on high to have compassion on you. For the LORD is a God of justice; how blessed are all those who long for Him.
> O people in Zion, inhabitant in Jerusalem, you will weep no longer. He will surely be gracious to you at the sound of your cry; when He hears it, He will answer you. Although the Lord has given you bread of privation and water of oppression, He, your Teacher will no longer hide Himself, but your eyes will behold your Teacher. Your ears will hear a word behind you, "This is the way, walk in it," whenever you turn to the right or to the left.

Do you notice what it says? He waits for us. He longs for us. He yearns to demonstrate His deep-seated compassion toward us. He comes running when He hears our voice! Perhaps we should tear out this passage of God's manual and carry it around with us. If He walks with us in such a manner, don't you think it would be a delight to Papa God's heart if we modeled the same activity with and toward Him?

Initiative is the issue. In the book of Acts, we don't see God following man, but rather man waiting on God and then trying to keep up with what God is doing. Then the equation gets all turned around, as the writer of the book of Mark indicates that these signs will follow those who believe (see Mark 16:17–18). So, who is following whom? Let's just put it this way: It takes two to tango!

Now, concerning the thread connected to the precedent of church history, let's close out this chapter by peering into the writings of Andrew Murray from his classic book *Waiting on God*. In it, he says:

> We must not only think of our waiting upon God, but also of what is more wonderful still, of God's waiting upon us. The vision of Him waiting on us will give new impulse and inspiration to our waiting upon Him. It will give us an unspeakable confidence that our waiting cannot be in vain. If He waits for us, then we may be sure that we are more than welcome—that He rejoices to find those He has been seeking for. Let us seek even now, at this moment, in the spirit of lowly waiting on God, to find out something of what it means. Therefore will the Lord wait, that He may be gracious unto you. We will accept and echo back the message: Blessed are all they that wait for Him.[1]

Keep on listening, just as the Lord listens to us. Keep on watching, even as the Lord keeps His eyes upon us. Be patient. Keep on waiting, just as Papa God is waiting for you. You will find Him when you do, and you will obtain favor from the Lord!

In the end, let us learn the valuable lessons of the ongoing activity of listening, waiting and watching. As we commit ourselves to these skills—these spiritual privileges—we will truly find Him, the Author of all life, and you will hear His endearing voice. Therefore, let us be alert and learn these sometimes lost arts of communion with our Master.

Father, in Jesus' great name, I thank You for graduate-level classes that are available for me in the School of the Spirit. Impart greater grace to me to enjoy these spiritual privileges. I count it an honor and blessing to be welcomed into Your presence and to sit at Your feet and listen to Your every word. Help me to be a good steward of these truths. Amen and amen!

THINK ABOUT IT

1. Choose one of the three principles of listening, watching and waiting contained in this chapter and write down in a personal journal what you have learned in this chapter about that lesson. Journaling is one of the best tools for retaining revelation. Ready? Now write!

2. Having taken these graduate-level classes in hearing God's voice today, what application are you going to bring into your life's experience? What spiritual discipline, or spiritual privilege, are you setting as a goal for your growth right now? Put feet to your faith now, applying your learning to real life!

11

Properly Responding to God's Voice

For He is God, and we are the people of His pasture and the sheep of His hand. Today, if you would hear His voice, do not harden your hearts.

Psalm 95:7–8

"Today if you hear His voice, do not harden your hearts, as when they provoked Me."

Hebrews 3:15

This command I entrust to you, Timothy, my son, in accordance with the prophecies previously made concerning you, that by them you fight the good fight.

1 Timothy 1:18

At some point, you may wonder, Why does there seem to be a delay to answered prayers? Or you may question, When is that promise from God ever going to come to pass? If you find yourself pondering these types of questions, you are definitely not alone. We all tend to live in what I call the "until clause," to one degree or another.

You see, there is hearing God's voice, and there is responding to God's voice. These are two interdependent sides of the same truth. Passivity is not even close to being a proper response to God and His word. God is moved by faith and by people who take action (see Daniel 11:32). We must be actively engaged in seeking the Lord for the conditions—whether spoken or not yet revealed—that must be met in order to unlock the promises He has given. This can take on a form of contending for the promised word to come to pass. In other words, there is the *promise revealed*, and then there is the *promise fulfilled*.

Isaiah 62:6–7 helps to reinforce this principle:

> On your walls, O Jerusalem, I have appointed watchmen; all day and all night they will never keep silent. You who remind the LORD, take no rest for yourselves; and give Him no rest until He establishes and makes Jerusalem a praise in the earth.

In between the two polar-opposite positions of the promise revealed and the promise fulfilled, there is the gap that I call the "until clause." In the above-quoted Isaiah passage, it appears that even God at times lives in an "until clause," waiting on us to fulfill our part of the equation.

So, how are we, as believers, supposed to respond in these transitional phases? We are not meant to stay in the valley, throw up our hands, resign, give up or just sit there. No! We must learn the ways of properly responding to the voice of God, thus contending for the promise in order to step into our Promised Land.

Learning from Biblical Precedents

Are biblical precedents given to us to study, perhaps as yet another part of our graduate-school curriculum? Of course! Let's take a glance at the life of Jacob first:

> Then Jacob was left alone, and a man wrestled with him until daybreak. When he saw that he had not prevailed against him, he touched the socket of his thigh; so the socket of Jacob's thigh was dislocated while he wrestled with him. Then he said, "Let me go, for the dawn is breaking." But he said, "I will not let you go unless you bless me." So he said to him, "What is your name?" And he said, "Jacob." He said, "Your name shall no longer be Jacob, but Israel; for you have striven with God and with men and have prevailed." Then Jacob asked him and said, "Please tell me your name." But he said, "Why is it that you ask my name?" And he blessed him there.
>
> Genesis 32:24–29

What is Jacob doing wrestling with an angel anyway? Why and what for? Some famous painters have depicted this scene relatively well over the years in their artwork. But is this just a nice, fabled Bible story to read to your kids or just another amazing piece of art? Is there a message in this depiction from the life of Jacob for us today?

I am convinced that there is in this story a dimension of contending for the promise for us to emulate. Many of us need more of this same tenacious attitude and gutsy approach when it comes to seeing the voiced promises of God fulfilled. It is my belief that our good, heavenly Father wants to bless us richly. He rewards diligence and faith. So, from a veteran, let me tell you: Do as Jacob did, and do not let go until you have received your inherited blessing!

Another biblical example—one of the best—comes from the lifestyle of prayer and prophetic response found in the ministry of Daniel. So, let's build on the lesson we learned from Jacob as we turn our attention to Daniel, a prophet living in exile in Babylonian captivity.

Daniel meditated on the promises revealed to Jeremiah that the Israelites' captivity would come to an end after seventy years of exile (see Daniel 9:1–2). Daniel responded to this promise of the Lord by praying to see if there were any hindrances standing in the way of their fulfillment. With that brief backdrop in mind, let's take a look at what happens next:

> Now while I was speaking and praying, and confessing my sin and the sin of my people Israel, and presenting my supplication before the LORD my God in behalf of the holy mountain of my God, while I was still speaking in prayer, then the man Gabriel, whom I had seen in the vision previously, came to me in my extreme weariness about the time of the evening offering. He gave me instruction and talked with me and said, "O Daniel, I have now come forth to give you insight with understanding. At the beginning of your supplications the command was issued, and I have come to tell you, for you are highly esteemed; so give heed to the message and gain understanding of the vision." . . .
>
> Then he said to me, "Do not be afraid, Daniel, for from the first day that you set your heart on understanding this and on humbling yourself before your God, your words were heard, and I have come in response to your words. But the prince of the kingdom of Persia was withstanding me for twenty-one days; then behold, Michael, one of the chief princes, came to help me, for I had been left there with the kings of Persia. Now I have come to give you an understanding of what will happen to your people in the latter days, for the vision pertains to the days yet future."
>
> Daniel 9:20–23; 10:12–14

In these biblical precedents from the lives of Jacob and Daniel, we find two different but complementary prerequisites. With

Jacob, we find tenacious contending. With Daniel, we find the opposite: humble contrition and the confessing of generational sins. We need to bring both of these stances together when we contend before the Lord so that the promises of God are brought forth in the here and now.

Why Contending Is Necessary

The following principles can be tools of understanding that help you keep moving forward, rather than getting stuck in a rut.

It's for More Than Just You

Realize that when you are contending for a breakthrough, you are doing this for more than just yourself. What you are going through is bigger than you! Every personal breakthrough is given so that you can turn around and impart to others that same faith, courage and whatever other grace package you just received from God. It is called multiplication, not just addition!

Your personal victory builds a testimony, which helps others receive strength and encouragement to persevere, too. You might just be contending for deliverance for your entire family, church culture, city and nation. Come on, now. You are contending for more than just yourself!

It Strengthens You in God

If you do CrossFit or some other workout regimen, you have a greater probability of looking buff. If you are a couch potato, then you will resemble one. In the ways of God, contending in the spiritual is a lot like lifting weights—there is a resistance factor that eventually works in your favor. Your tenacious response causes you to grow up spiritually, tests your motivations and builds you up.

The process of becoming might seem intense at times, but, believe me, it strengthens you in the long run. Contending builds you up!

It Threatens the Enemy

Why is contending necessary? Because we have a real enemy, and your success is a threat to the kingdom of darkness. Your fulfilled dream is one of the enemy's worst nightmares!

You must put on the full armor of God (see Ephesians 6:10–17) because your wrestling match is not against your boss, spouse, pastor or children. It is against evil demonic powers arrayed against you, your promise and God's purposes.

Our battle is against the powers, principalities of darkness and evils spirits in the heavenly places. We were born in the middle of a great cosmic war between the forces of good and evil, and as believers in Christ Jesus, we were born to be effective spiritual warriors. It is up to us to enforce the victory Jesus Christ won on Calvary.

It Keeps the Promise Going

Reality check! Apart from of the empowering work of the Holy Spirit, man is weak and frail. Often, the fulfillment of the Lord's prophetic invitations does not just depend on us; it involves the will, attitude and fortitude of others. Some people, some churches, some cities and some nations just give up too soon. When they are at the brink of crossing over from promises revealed to promises fulfilled, they quit.

Not on my watch! I have seen promises of revival or break-through for entire cities dropped by one generation, only for another generation to rise up later and pick up the dropped promise until it is birthed in earth as it is in heaven.

In all honesty, we all fail from time to time. But then God, strong in mercy and loving-kindness, comes through, revives us again and calls others to step up to the plate alongside us. Believe me, I know this drill. Contending is essential because we live and walk with weak, frail people.

How to Keep Moving

Contending for a promise long after it has been released involves perseverance. Believe me, I know. At times, it takes all of the strength we have to continue. But we must never, never quit! With this in mind, here are some ways I have found to keep going when this road grows long.

Walk in Faith

All progress in the Christian life is made through faith. This is a truth for people of all ages, of every background, of every gift mix and at all times! We walk by faith and not by sight (see 2 Corinthians 5:7). Also, God is a rewarder of those who diligently seek Him, and He rewards faith (see Hebrews 11:6).

So, take one more step. Then take another step. It is a walk—not a sprint—of faith. For Jesus' sake, and for the sake of others, just don't stop.

Receive and Release

This is a big one. Want to move forward in your personal or corporate destiny in God? Want to see that promise come to pass, the one that came to you on that crystal-clear morning through that whisper of the Holy Spirit? Then realize you are part of a relational community—or, at least, you should be. This means that you must learn to receive God's great love, grace and forgiveness and then turn around and demonstrate that same upside-down Kingdom to others.

Resentment and bitterness are hindrances that must be identified and removed through the power of forgiveness before the manifestation will come tumbling forth. On this subject, I was given a very short, clear dream one morning that has stuck with me ever since. I heard the voice of God clearly state, *We are never too old for the Sermon on the Mount.* Do you know what the Sermon on the Mount says on this subject? It says to be merciful, and you will receive mercy (see Matthew 5:7).

Belong to Others

Okay, here is another principle that deals with our relationship with the Body of Christ: We need each other! We need the friendship, prayers, encouragement and strength others can give us, and it only comes by walking with them.

According to 1 John 5:4, "For whatever is born of God overcomes the world; and this is the victory that has overcome the world—our faith." Note that this verse does not say "my faith." It states "our faith." At times, you may need my faith added to your faith. In my life, there have been times I certainly needed the faith of others to be joined to my faith so I could overcome. We overcome the world by our faith.

Again, I cannot overemphasize this. If you were to know my journey over the last decade-plus, you would know it has not been a cakewalk. I endured three bouts of non-Hodgkin's cancer over a nine-year period and lost my dear wife and the mother of our four kids to colon cancer, all at the same time. Believe me, I needed others to hold up my arms, just like Moses needed Aaron and Hur (see Exodus 17:11–12). I needed my family. I needed my church family. I also needed, and still need, a few good close-mouthed intercessors. So do you!

Behold His Face

It is a love war that we are engaged in. Look into God's face. Get yourself in front of Him. How do we continue? By engaging in the art of beholding. You become like what or whom you behold. When I look into the mirror of God's Word, it strengthens me and draws me into a deeper, more passionate pursuit of God. Since God is an equal-opportunity employer, He will do this for you, as well.

Obedience to the Holy Spirit's voice is as much about being transformed into the image of the Son as it is about receiving the answer or promise we seek. Continue on the journey of earnest longings. Gaze into the beauty of the Lord. Cry out for greater intimacy with Christ.

Sacrifice to Release Power

Today's sacrifice releases tomorrow's privilege and provision. Today's humility releases greater grace for your future (see James 4:6). What you do matters, and how you live determines your outcome. So stretch yourself in prayer, love, fasting and acts of kindness.

If you wait to begin tithing when you think you can afford it, you never will. Giving is an enormous blessing and opportunity to partner with the God who supplies. Sow some sacrificial seeds of your time, money and talents in faith, and watch God move in your behalf! Little acts of sacrifice release heaven's response.

Pursue Fresh Vision

According to Proverbs 29:18, without a progressive vision, the people perish. Are you keeping God first? Are you seeking first His kingdom and His righteousness (see Matthew 6:33)? Are you keeping the authentic, confirmed, revealed promise in front of your eyes? With renewed, revelatory vision, you are strengthened in your resolve and receive grace for the journey.

We each are in need of renewed vision. Such vision has sustained me through the valleys and dry seasons of life. At those times, I turn to my journals and rehearse the words that the Holy Spirit has spoken to me in the past. Then, in worship and prayer, I wait in His presence with eager anticipation for His confirming voice to speak to me. I listen for more insight to be granted.

Steward It by Journaling

Do you need assistance retaining what you have received? There is a simple solution for you—journaling! Yes, it is another one of those spiritual privileges we have mentioned earlier. Journaling is a tried-and-tested spiritual tool for stewarding revelation. It is a tool that can aid you in discerning the voice of the Holy Spirit.

In this case, journaling is a form of recording a summary of the content and the times and places the Holy Spirit speaks to you, for future reference. God speaks to His children much of the time! However, we do not always differentiate His voice from our own thoughts, and thus we are hesitant to take action on what we have heard. If we record what He is speaking, though, we will eventually notice confirmations of His voice and word. Thus, we will be enabled to walk out God's words to us with greater confidence. Journaling then becomes a way of sorting God's thoughts from our own.

I have kept many different types of journals over the years. After Michal Ann passed away, I simply recorded my thoughts, feelings and emotions for the first year. I titled this *The Journal of Searching Man*. After one year, I closed out that journal and shifted to *The Journal of a Hopeful Man*. Other journals of mine are summaries of significant dreams and visions I have received.

One of the greatest treasures I possess to this day is Michal Ann's handwritten journals. I found the one she used in 1993, which included the incredible nine straight weeks of nightly visitations she received. Am I ever glad she journaled! I can look back on those encounters and receive faith, hope and love from them.

Many believers have found this simple act of recording revelations to be one of the strategic missing links in their journey of hearing and discerning the voice of God. The continuity of language that emerges, the divine suggestions they notice and the art of interpreting symbols that occurs only matures as we grow in our journaling experience. Just get started and do it. It will serve you well as a proper response to hearing the voice of God.

Lean in to Perseverance

Lastly, just don't quit! I have a piercing word printed on a card from my late wife. It was her last word given to our family and myself by an actual angel of the Lord. On the front of the card, it states, "Never, never, never, never give up!" The inside of the card reads, "I will never, never, never stop cheering for you."

I carry that card with me in my Bible everywhere I go. I keep it close to my heart. At times, life's circumstances can seem so overwhelming. I became a single dad to four. I went into hundreds of thousands of dollars' worth of medical debt. But I have a word from the voice of God: Don't quit!

And so I say to you: Persevere. It will pay off. The promise will come. You will move from promise revealed to promise fulfilled. Just don't quit. If I had one key in life, it would be called old-fashioned perseverance, and I want that same key to be in your possession, too.

What You Can Know for Sure

In order to succeed in life and ministry, some basic, fundamental decisions must be applied every time—no matter what. These basic wisdom decisions fall into the categories of yes and no. You can never go wrong by sticking close to these basics.

Say Yes to the Lord

1. Focus your faith on the Giver, not the gift (see Hebrews 11:6).
2. Hold on to the words God has given with "open expectancy."
3. Be thankful for what you have received. We are not to despise God's words (see 1 Thessalonians 5:20).
4. Follow Daniel's example and pray the promise into existence (see Jeremiah 29:10; Daniel 9).
5. Fight the good fight of faith—do spiritual battle according to the word from the Lord (see 1 Timothy 1:18).

Say No to Ourselves

1. Put down fantasy and unrestrained speculation, and bring every thought captive to Christ Jesus (see 2 Corinthians 10:5).
2. Embrace discipleship and the death-and-resurrection process (see John 12:24).
3. Embrace patience! There are no shortcuts with God.
4. Learn to give grace and mercy to others, as we are all still in training.

How to Respond to Dry Seasons

At times, we can become frustrated with this whole business of hearing and responding to the voice of God. Perhaps it happens because of disappointment or unfulfilled expectations. There can be multiple reasons we grow weary of taking class after class in the School of the Spirit to learn how to hear God's voice today. If you have ever found yourself in such a place, then consider some of the following proper responses to your dry season:

1. Stick with what you already know. Ask yourself, *What was the last thing the Lord said?*
2. Consider that you might be in a test. Will you pass it?
3. Don't doubt in darkness what you have seen or heard in times of light.
4. Don't compare yourself to others.
5. Be childlike . . . don't overly complicate things!

Wow! We covered a lot of material in this one chapter alone. It makes me realize I could compose an entire book on this one subject. Mercy! But I trust that these thoughts and principles, gleaned from many years of experience in my own life and ministry, will be useful tools for you as you grow in your ability to properly respond to the voice of God.

Father God, I am grateful for the progress we are making together. Thank You for enrolling me in these graduate-level classes on hearing and discerning Your voice. Help me to properly respond to Your whispers, dreams, visitations and various encounters. I want to listen and obey! Lead me by Your grace into greater applications of these spiritual privileges. In Jesus' great name, Amen.

THINK ABOUT IT

1. What are some of the requirements for moving forward in hearing God's voice today? Why is contending for the promise you have heard necessary?

2. Have you ever journaled? If so, recite an example where journaling was beneficial. How was it used to bring confirmation in your life? If you have not journaled before, consider starting now.

12

At the End of the Day

You have taken account of my wanderings; put my tears in Your bottle. Are they not in Your book? Then my enemies will turn back in the day when I call; this I know, that God is for me.

Psalm 56:8–9

Not that I have already obtained it or have already become perfect, but I press on so that I may lay hold of that for which also I was laid hold of by Christ Jesus. Brethren, I do not regard myself as having laid hold of it yet; but one thing I do: forgetting what lies behind and reaching forward to what lies ahead, I press on toward the goal for the prize of the upward call of God in Christ Jesus.

Philippians 3:12–14

> I have fought the good fight, I have finished the
> course, I have kept the faith.
>
> 2 Timothy 4:7

> Morning by morning he wakens me and opens my
> understanding to his will. The Sovereign LORD has
> spoken to me, and I have listened.
>
> Isaiah 50:4–5 NLT

God chooses each one of us to fulfill a distinct purpose and destiny in Him. The call of Jesus causes us to cast away the "fishing nets" (see Matthew 4:18–22) of the things that are familiar to us to become pilgrims on a journey. Like Jesus' first disciples, we don't know what the future holds. Christ helps us to be determined, no matter the cost, to run hard to follow Him in order to fulfill His will.

We struggle at times and we get frustrated, tempted to throw in the towel, but we continue. The once-bright pathway temporarily disappears. We thought we had heard our Master say where we were headed. Yet by sight, we can seemingly appear to be no further down the road than when we first began.

In this particular subject, I can honestly say, "I resemble that statement!" I never thought my life would take all the twists and turns that it has. My dear, late wife, Michal Ann, graduated to be with Jesus in the fall of 2008. I endured nine years of non-Hodgkin's lymphoma cancer. Our promised "field of dreams" seemed more like a "field of land mines." At times, it felt like I was living an old country song from the town I live in—Nashville, Tennessee. Even my dog, who slept in our room for fourteen years, died. Yet like the great gospel singer Andraé Crouch, I can truly sing, "Through it all, I have learned to trust in Jesus. I have learned to trust in God." I am still singing that tune, and I will until my last breath.

We can learn many great lessons from believers who have gone before us. I learned an amazing truth from my spiritual grandfather in the faith, Derek Prince. When I was a young man and the cement in the foundation of my life was still wet, I heard this wise British Bible teacher say with much sass, "All progress in the Christian life is by faith, and God has no plans on changing His ways!"

We need to turn to our road map over and over again. We lean our ear in His direction to receive encouragement for today. Yes, it may be an arduous path, but it is indeed an adventure. We must proceed. The requirements: hearing God's voice and obeying it.

Has God Said?

The enemy attempts his same old tricks, one after another. How often have we heard God speak clearly, only to have it followed by the devil's sly comeback, "Has God *really* said?"—which is the same question the serpent asked Eve in the Garden (see Genesis 3:1). The enemy has repeated those words in the ear of every person who has ever tried to follow the Lord God.

Undermining the word of the Lord is one of the enemy's main ploys. Unless we have God's Word rooted deeply inside us, we can easily get off the track because of Satan's insinuations. Vaguely trying to quote God's Word, we repeat Eve's mistake: "Don't eat—in fact, don't even touch it!" In fact, Eve added the last phrase about not touching it (see Genesis 3:3). God had not forbidden touching the fruit (see Genesis 2:16–17).

Like Eve, we misquote God, and we are sometimes caught off balance. Proverbs 30:5–6 warns us, "Every word of God is tested; He is a shield to those who take refuge in Him. Do not add to His words or He will reprove you, and you will be proved a liar."

Many of us struggle to know whether we actually heard God. But that was not the case with Adam and Eve. There was no doubt that God had spoken to them. So the serpent's strategy bypassed the question of whether God had spoken; he questioned God's intent. The enemy appears to know the Word rather well, so he distorts it subtly, a little here and there, often without our even realizing it. It will happen to you: When the devil cannot stop you from hearing God's word, He moves on to another strategy of distorting the goodness of God Himself.

I wish Eve had stood firm: "Yes, that's what God said! God is good, and He knows what I need. I'm not going to listen to snakes!" Now, I am not an Eve-basher; I just want us to learn all we can in order to avoid similar pitfalls. And, yes, how about Adam's response? Maybe he should have talked to his lady and protected her from that snake to start with! Remember, Isaiah said, "All we like sheep have gone astray; we have turned, every one, to his own way" (Isaiah 53:6 NKJV).

Line of Fire

Sometimes we feel as though we are the direct target of spiritual warfare. It is because we are ambassadors of One who has vanquished all the collective forces of the dark side. We may not be the direct targets, but we may be the most visible ones. The devil lost his battle of coming against God Himself, so he shifted tactics and started going after those whom God loves. But there is victory when we walk in our Kingdom birthright.

Therefore, like Jesus, our Messiah, in the Garden of Gethsemane, we kneel before our Lord and Maker, and we receive grace and strength for the battle. Putting on the full armor of God, we arm ourselves for the fight. Challenges, doubts, fears and questions come at us from multiple directions. Taking up the shield of faith, we extinguish the fiery darts of the evil one. Standing confident in God's spoken and confirmed word, we wage war against the spirits of wickedness and deception.

Submitted to God, we resist the devil, who must flee from us (see James 4:7). We rise with the high praises of God in our mouths, driving the deceiver farther away with our worship. I can just see that accuser right now—he is backing away, sticking his fingers in his ears every time one of God's kids lifts up the sacrifice of praise!

We must hear and adhere to the voice of God. The enemy tries to snatch the word away. We must hang on to it. Somewhere in there, we begin to realize that maybe God's goal is something more than merely giving us another word.

Have you ever felt like the Word got a hold of you? He is the Living Word.

Tested by the Word

"The words of the LORD are pure words; as silver tried in a furnace on the earth, refined seven times" (Psalm 12:6).

Often, when we receive an exciting revelation from God, He uses the revelation itself to test us and purify us so that our character will be able to convey the word to others. I wonder how Joseph felt as he endured trials and testing, pits and prisons, because of his two life-shaping dreams. It took many years for him to see the fulfillment of those words.

I wonder how Abram felt when the Lord told him to move from his familiar surroundings to a strange land. Would he listen and obey, leave his country and follow Yahweh? If so, God said He would bless him with a lineage as numerous as the stars of the sky. Years of testing transpired, as Abraham believed God. He had to be convinced that the voice that had spoken to him was not a crazy notion in his head.

I imagine that his first step of obedience, packing up and moving to Haran, was the hardest one of all. When he took that first step, believing he had heard God, he found that taking another step would not be so hard. Eventually his trail of hearing and obeying brought him to the land of promise, only to find the land suffering from severe famine.

Along the way, his failures reflected his capitulation to Satan's ploys, but they did not disqualify him. He attempted to produce an heir through Hagar, trying to fulfill God's word in his own strength and understanding. All the trials prepared Abraham for his ultimate test of faith—being asked to sacrifice his own miraculously conceived son, the son of his old age (see Genesis 22). Abraham, by now a giant in faith, believed that if need be, God would raise his son Isaac up from the dead to fulfill His promise!

These trials were all a part of the necessary steps of faith that Abraham needed to take. Many years later, he saw God's promises fulfilled, with accompanying struggles, trials, testing—and a refining of God's word.

All through the Bible, we see the long journeys of those who heard from God in one radical way or another. Consider Moses. How many seemingly endless years did he faithfully follow God's voice?

Or the little shepherd boy David—how many years after he received his word from God did he become king? How many times was he tested by the question, Did God really say that? How many times did he wonder if Samuel had been right? How many times was he pressured by his own men to fulfill God's word by his own strength?

Each of these had received a promise, but when the testing of those words came, these men of God responded differently to God's words and to the subsequent testings. All of them failed along the way. But God used their failures as part of their character-development process. Even our failures can be used to help keep God's word pure.

What Is Your Response?

Should we be exceptions to this pattern? If we can hear God's voice and have been called to even a small task in building His Kingdom, let's rejoice that we have been found worthy to be called God's children and to be tested on the very promises He gives to us.

God will not allow us to be tested beyond what we can bear (see 1 Corinthians 10:13). He is a loving Father who wants to see His children succeed. He simply allows trials in our life so that we will have the proven character needed to carry the message: "We also exult in our tribulations, knowing that tribulation brings about perseverance; and perseverance, proven character; and proven character, hope; and hope does not disappoint" (Romans 5:3–5).

God tests His very words on purpose so that we will reach our hand heavenward to grasp His hand of mercy and grace. He is a good Father. He wants us to grow up to be as much like His Son as we can be. Although we may find it difficult to comprehend His mysterious ways, we can be sure of *His* character, which is good through and through. God is good all the time, and His mercies are new every morning.

How many times have I allowed God's word to slip away because I thought the testings were simply evidence that I had heard it wrong? How many times did I lose out when the little voice said, *Did God* really *say that?*

Ministry to the Nations

Years ago, I was the pastor of a small congregation in a college town in Missouri. I was dedicated to my flock but restless on the inside. Healing evangelist Mahesh Chavda came to minister to our congregation, and at the end of the service, I felt an urge to go and pull on his coattails as if I were drawing forth an anointing from him. So I took hold of his suit jacket, and a strong current of God's power overwhelmed me. The next thing I knew, I was lying on the platform!

Lying there under the power of God, I began to see a vision. I could see a man's hand with a globe rotating in it. A sort of ticker tape with words on it came before my sight, listing the names of nation after nation. I could read the list of nations clearly as they rushed before my mind: Guatemala, Haiti, Israel—on and on. I was stunned and wondered what all this meant. At that point in my life, I had only been outside of the United States one time.

Then a word came to me: *You cannot perceive and receive this in your natural mind, because in your natural mind there is self-doubt. You can only perceive and receive this in your spirit through faith.* The Holy Spirit continued to hover over me, and a second time I saw the same vision. A globe was turning in a man's hand, and names of nations circulated before my eyes.

I began to analyze what was happening, skeptical that it could be from God. But the voice came to me a second time, clearly whispering the exact same words, convicting my heart as the words settled deep down inside of me: *You cannot perceive and receive this in your natural mind, because in your natural mind there is self-doubt. You can only perceive and receive this in your spirit through faith.*

I tried to get up but was unsuccessful. It was as if the Holy Spirit had set a rock on my chest to make sure that I could not move until I got the picture. The vision occurred a third time: a globe revolving in a man's hand with the list of the nations. By now, the names of the nations were burning in my heart.

As the words began to settle deep within me, something more transpired. Faith was awakened inside of me. God spoke other things to me as I lay there—promises from His throne and conditions that had to be met.

Finally, His presence began to lift from me. I sat up. I was dazed. I arose. I was changed, and I believed what God had promised. I had very little understanding of what this meant, the cost it would entail or any other details. But I knew that I knew that I knew that I was born for a ministry to the nations. A little skinny boy from Cowgill, Missouri, was going to be sent to the nations for such a time as this.

I learned years ago to kneel on the promises. That means I pray such promises back into the Father's hearing. It brings such words to life to pray them into being! Today this is often termed *prophetic intercession.*

By the grace of God, I have now ministered in every one of the nations revealed to me that day—and at the time of this writing, several more. God told me that He would give to me the blessing of John Wesley—that the world would be my parish. I have crisscrossed well over fifty nations and have publications translated in well over twenty different languages. God's word to me has been true—it has been so.

I cannot spell out all the second-guessing I have been through, the sleepless nights, the wrestling against the demonic hosts, the cost of leaving family and friends to move to another state just because God said so, the loneliness of leaving my family behind to go out and do the Master's call. Michal Ann and I picked up our cross many times to walk out that word and several others. But we always knew we were in good company, following in others' footsteps.

Today, I have another price I pay. Right now, I walk alone. Yet even this is another opportunity to find hope in Christ, because there really is a silver lining that comes with every storm cloud.

It is worth the price—to hear His voice, to know His kiss, to sense His touch. Satisfaction does not come as much through finishing a task as it does through increased intimacy with Him. He is my journey's beginning—and its end. Yes, at the end of the day, I long to hear those words: *Well done, My faithful son. Well done!*

This Is My Father's World

When I first penned these words in this final chapter, my entire being was overwhelmed with the loveliness of God's presence. I had just come back in from my southern-facing front porch, which overlooked the beautiful hills of Franklin, Tennessee. The sun was setting, and the sky was ignited with a display of heavenly colors.

In gratitude to God, I lifted my glass and gave God a toast: "To the promises of God and to the God who promises!" With tears of gratitude, I then sang this old hymn to Him. Singing is one of those sweet spots for me. If I am down, I just worship my way out of it! So read these familiar words, and sing them if you know the tune:

> This is my Father's world,
> And to my listening ears
> All nature sings, and round me rings
> The music of the spheres.
> This is my Father's world:
> I rest me in the thought
> Of rocks and trees, of skies and seas;
> His hand the wonders wrought.
>
> This is my Father's world,
> The birds their carols raise,
> The morning light, the lily white,

Declare their Maker's praise.
This is my Father's world,
He shines in all that's fair;
In the rustling grass I hear him pass;
He speaks to me everywhere.

This is my Father's world,
O let me ne'er forget
That though the wrong seems oft so strong,
God is the ruler yet.
This is my Father's world,
Why should my heart be sad?
The Lord is King; let the heavens ring!
God reigns; let the earth be glad![1]

Do you hear Him speaking now to you? He is waiting to have a moment just with you. Lean your head a bit and you will hear more than words. You will hear the sound of love beating in His heart. He is your journey's end. At the end of the day, knowing God is what hearing God is ultimately all about! Oh, how I love Jesus, because He first loved me!

In the amazing name of Jesus, I declare that God is good all the time and that all things work together for good. I love the sound of Your voice, Lord; it brings such joy and comfort to me. Yes, I come to the garden alone, and the joy we share while we tarry there, none other has ever known. Give me more lessons in the School of the Spirit to better hear and discern Your voice. By grace, I make a commitment to obey Your Word and release the fragrance of Christ wherever I go. What a honor and privilege it is to hear Your voice today. Amen and amen!

THINK ABOUT IT

1. What is the major lesson you have learned from this chapter that you desire to bring as an application into your life?

2. At the end of the day, we each want to listen and obey the voice of God. At the conclusion of the reading of this book, what purpose or destiny do you sense the Holy Spirit has confirmed to you concerning your life? Bring that in prayer to the Lord, and ask for His assistance in doing His will.

Notes

Chapter 1: As It Was in the Beginning

1. Mark Virkler, quoted in Leonard LeSourd, ed., *Touching the Heart of God* (Old Tappan, N.J.: Chosen Books, 1990), 59.

2. Dutch Sheets, quoted in Quin Sherrer, *Listen, God Is Speaking to You* (Ann Arbor, Mich.: Vine Books, 1999), 9.

3. James W. Goll, *The Coming Prophetic Revolution* (Grand Rapids, Mich.: Chosen Books, 2001), 28.

4. Fuchsia Pickett, *Receiving Divine Revelation* (Lake Mary, Fla.: Creation House, 1977), 15.

Chapter 2: The Holy Spirit at Work Today

1. Quin Sherrer and Ruthanne Garlock, *The Beginner's Guide to Receiving the Holy Spirit* (Ann Arbor, Mich.: Vine Books, 2002), 45.

2. David Wilkerson, "What It Means to Walk in the Spirit," Times Square Church Pulpit Series, August 15, 1994, http://www.tscpulpitseries.org/english /1990s/ts940815.html.

3. *Merriam-Webster's Collegiate Dictionary,* 11th edition, s.v. "tutor."

Chapter 3: The Sound of Many Rushing Waters

1. James W. Goll, *The Coming Prophetic Revolution* (Grand Rapids, Mich.: Chosen Books, 2001), 125.

2. Sherrer, *Listen, God Is Speaking to You*, 26.

3. Ibid., 25–26.

Chapter 4: Walking in Our Kingdom Birthright

1. Jack Deere, *Surprised by the Power of the Spirit* (Grand Rapids, Mich.: Zondervan, 1993), 212.

2. James W. Goll, *The Coming Prophetic Revolution* (Grand Rapids, Mich.: Chosen Books, 2001), 19–20.

3. Michael Brown, *Revolution! The Call to Holy War* (Ventura, Calif.: Renew, 2000), 57–58.

4. Sam Storms, *The Beginner's Guide to Spiritual Gifts* (Ann Arbor, Mich.: Vine Books, 2002), 17–18.

Chapter 5: Built upon the Rock

1. *Vine's Expository Dictionary of New Testament Words* (Old Tappan, N.J.: Fleming H. Revel Company, 1966), 230.

2. James W. Goll, *The Lost Art of Practicing His Presence* (Shippensburg, Pa.: Destiny Image, 2005), 130–131.

3. Peter Toon, *Meditating as a Christian* (London: HarperCollins, 1991), 61.

4. Richard Foster, *Prayer: Finding the Heart's True Home* (San Francisco: HarperSanFrancisco, 1992), 146.

Chapter 6: Ten Practical, Personal Tools

1. The content of this chapter has been greatly inspired by, though not directly quoted from, the outstanding book *Is That Really You, God?* by Loren Cunningham. Loren Cunningham is the founder of Youth With A Mission. I would highly recommend this book to anyone desiring to learn more about hearing and discerning the voice of God. Used by permission.

Chapter 7: Walking in Community

1. Jim Goll and Michal Ann Goll, *Encounters with a Supernatural God* (Shippensburg, Pa.: Destiny Image, 1998), 2.

2. Ibid., 13.

3. James W. Goll, *Prophetic Foundations* (Franklin, Tenn.: Ministry to the Nations, 2000), 35.

4. James W. Goll, *The Coming Prophetic Revolution* (Grand Rapids, Mich.: Chosen Books, 2001), 28.

Chapter 8: Hearing with Discernment

1. C. Peter Wagner, *Discover Your Spiritual Gifts* (Minneapolis: Chosen, 2012), as quoted in James W. Goll, *Impacting the World through Spiritual Gifts* (New Kensington, Pa.: Whitaker House, 2016), 47–48.

2. Sam Storms, *The Beginner's Guide to Spiritual Gifts* (Ann Arbor, Mich.: Vine Books, 2002), 103–104.

Chapter 10: Listening, Waiting and Watching

1. Andrew Murray, *Waiting on God* (New Kensington, Pa.: Whitaker House, 1981), 87.

Chapter 12: At the End of the Day

1. Maltbie Davenport Babcock, "This Is My Father's World," words 1901, public domain.

Recommended Reading

Cunningham, Loren. *Is That Really You, Lord?* 2nd ed. Seattle: YWAM Publishing, 2001.

Deere, Jack. *Surprised by the Voice of God*. Revised edition. Grand Rapids, Mich.: Zondervan Publishing House, 1998.

Jacobs, Cindy. *The Voice of God*. Minneapolis: Chosen Books, 2004.

Prince, Derek. *How to Judge Prophecy*. Charlotte, N.C.: Derek Prince Publications, 1971.

Sherrer, Quin. *Listen, God Is Speaking to You*. Ann Arbor, Mich.: Vine Books, 1999.

Virkler, Mark. *Communion with God*. Shippensburg, Pa.: Destiny Image, 1991.

Dr. James W. Goll is the founder of God Encounters, formerly called Encounters Network, based in Franklin, Tennessee. He is also the founder of Prayer Storm and and the author of numerous books, study guides and classes. He is a certified Life Language trainer and CEO of Goll Ideation LLC. James is a member of the Harvest International Ministries apostolic team and an instructor in the Wagner Leadership Institute. He is a consultant to ministries around the world. His chief desire is to win for the Lamb the rewards for His suffering.

After pastoring in the Midwest, James was thrust into the role of an equipper and trainer internationally. He has traveled extensively to every continent, carrying a passion for Jesus wherever he goes. He desires to see the Body of Christ become a house of prayer for all nations and be empowered by the Holy Spirit to spread the Good News to every country and to all peoples.

James and Michal Ann Goll were married for more than 32 years before her graduation to heaven in the fall of 2008. They have four wonderful adult children, all of whom are now married, and James is now "Gramps" to a growing number of grandchildren. He makes his home in the southern charm of Franklin, Tennessee.

For more information:
James W. Goll
God Encounters
P.O. Box 1653
Franklin, TN 37065
Phone: 615-599-5552 *or* 1-877-200-1604

Website:
www.godencounters.com *or* www.jamesgoll.com

Email:
info@godencounters.com *or* invite@godencounters.com